'How could Hungary become a willing laboratory for Orbán's corrupt populist autocracy and illiberalism? This excellent book fills a crucial gap in the literature, offering a rare empirical analysis of how Hungarians think about the law, politics and their nation. Tribalism and populism represent a mortal threat for liberal democracies, and we urgently need to understand why voters succumb to radical illiberal ideologies. This book is a must-read for anyone interested in politics, law, psychology and social issues, and will be of interest to researchers, students and practitioners in all areas of the social sciences.'

Professor Joe Forgas, *Scientia Professor, University of New South Wales, Sydney*

Changing Legal and Civic Culture in an Illiberal Democracy

Changing Legal and Civic Culture in an Illiberal Democracy is a unique empirical study on recent developments in legal and civic consciousness in Hungary. Drawing its methodology from social psychology, this book illuminates a shift in legal consciousness during the time in which Orbán's government has cemented Hungary's reputation as an illiberal democracy.

The book foregrounds the voices of the Hungarian population in how they view the shift toward increasingly right-wing politics and an erosion of the rule of law. It opens with an extensive theoretical introduction of the historical development and psychological dimensions of legal consciousness in Hungary and relates the Hungarian research to international developments. It then presents its empirical results and offers a jargon-free account of ordinary people's changing perceptions of their relationship to Hungary's civic and legal cultures, before finally examining the correlations between surveys. Methodologically, the book establishes that theories of legal consciousness and social change are bolstered by empirical data.

Offering a new way of approaching shifts in legal consciousness and the rule of law in Balkan and Eastern European countries, this book will be of great interest to researchers and students of social psychology, law, international relations and Central European studies.

István H. Szilágyi is Professor of Law at Pázmány Péter Catholic University, Budapest, Hungary.

László Kelemen is a practicing Attorney at Law, who took a PhD in Psychology from the University of Pécs in 2014, Hungary. He is the author of two books in the area of law and psychology.

Sam Gilchrist Hall is Senior Lecturer in English at Károli Gáspár University, Budapest, and Visiting Lecturer at the Central European University, Vienna.

Changing Legal and Civic Culture in an Illiberal Democracy

A Social Psychological Survey of the Hungarian Legal System

**István H. Szilágyi,
László Kelemen and
Sam Gilchrist Hall**

Translated by Tamás Juhász

LONDON AND NEW YORK

First published 2022
by Routledge
2 Park Square, Milton Park, Abingdon, Oxon OX14 4RN

and by Routledge
605 Third Avenue, New York, NY 10158

Routledge is an imprint of the Taylor & Francis Group, an informa business

Translated by Tamás Juhász

British Library Cataloguing-in-Publication Data
A catalogue record for this book is available from the British Library

Library of Congress Cataloging-in-Publication Data
A catalog record for this book has been requested

ISBN: 978-1-032-03769-1 (hbk)
ISBN: 978-1-032-03773-8 (pbk)
ISBN: 978-1-003-18892-6 (ebk)

Typeset in Times New Roman
by Apex CoVantage, LLC

We do not see the world as it is but as we are.

– Epictetus

Neither the future nor the past weighs on you; it is always the present.

– Marcus Aurelius

Contents

Tables and figures

Figures

Tables

Acknowledgments

István H. Szilágyi and László Kelemen wish to thank the latter's former supervisor, the late János László, and József Forgács for their help in the formative and later stages of the project. During the related survey of law students, Miklós Hollán was a coauthor and we would like to extend our gratitude to him. Special thanks are also due to Tamás Juhász, from whose meticulous attention to detail in the translation the project benefited immeasurably. We extend our collective thanks to György Gajduschek, Balázs Fekete and Zoltán Fleck for sharing their expertise, while Zoltán Előd Tóth's high standards in methodological matters provided us with indispensable guidelines. We are also all especially grateful the two anonymous reviewers for Routledge, whose comments helped immensely in clarifying the aims and scope of this book. This book is dedicated to the late Professor János László.

The last significant representative of stoic philosophy, Marcus Aurelius, reminds to remain open and listen attentively to others and his words, we believe, ring truer than ever:

> "If anyone can point out convincingly that judgment or behavior is erroneous, I am quite willing to change my course of action because what I search is the truth and the truth has never hurt anyone. However, if you stubbornly insist on your error and ignorance, you hurt yourself".

István H. Szilágyi, László Kelemen and
Sam Gilchrist Hall

1 Introduction

Changing Legal and Civic Culture in an Illiberal Democracy: A Social Psychological Survey of the Hungarian Legal System is premised on the idea that shifts in individual perceptions of social reality can provide us with a verifiable way of understanding social change in a country that has attracted considerable international attention in recent years. We feel it is important to understand such shifts by scaling the statistics resulting from our surveys of the Hungarian population in 2010 and 2018 and presenting them in an intelligible way for the general reader, rather than resorting to hyperbolic condemnation of the Orbán regime, characteristic of much of the international coverage of Hungary, or by launching debate about the erosion of civil society into the stratosphere of academic theorization.

This book is part of a longer project that was launched 12 years ago. In 2007, we surveyed the attitude of full-time law students toward crime, criminal justice and law enforcement, and in 2010, we compared and analyzed differences between the attitudes of a representative sample comprising 1,000 people and one comprising 100 lawyers. These studies focused on certain psychological characteristics, such as alienation, self-esteem, modes of thought, open/closed mindedness and the need for autocracy, while attitudes toward the duality of globalism and parochialism were also explored. Five years later, in 2012, the survey was repeated, and we compared the findings of the two studies. The present volume is, likewise, a sequel to the study based on the representative sample of the general population. All four studies are essentially longitudinal in character. This method provides, we believe, an empirically verifiable worm's-eye view of how the population's perception of society and their role within it has changed in eight short years.

1.1 What kind of research is behind this book?

All three previous publications were billed as "social psychological research" in their subtitles and the present volume continues with this approach. Of course, psychology covers a large number of fields and methodologies, and reflects the tradition of thinking about society in two basic ways. One approach is societally centered, while the other is focused on the individual. The former emphasizes the primacy of groups, institutions and social structures over individuals, whereas the other assumes primacy of individual processes and functions over these societal aspects. Social psychology tends toward examining the world in broader social terms, for it studies social relations and the interaction *between* individuals. Our study explores opinions about and attitudes toward legal and political institutions in Hungary. It is, in other words, classical attitudinal research. Attitudes derive from acts of evaluation with cognitive, affective and behavioral components. But why are such subjective attitudes so important? Well, attitudes, rightly or wrongly held, manifest themselves in behavior toward others, while for an individual, attitudes define perception, thought and even physical behavior. If we know the attitude of others on an interpersonal level, the world opens up for us, and when it comes to interactions between groups, our attitudes toward our groups and toward other groups play a key role in cooperation, conflict and competition. Perhaps the greatest strength of this attitudinal approach, however, lies in the fact that it does not impose particular theories on people, but rather allows their options to speak for themselves.

Social psychological research has three basic types – descriptive, correlational and experimental – and our study is correlational. Correlational research does not identify causal relations; instead, it wants to establish correlations between two factors linked to the same, psychologically relevant phenomenon. To describe these methodologies in more detail, it is necessary to distinguish between strategies of social psychological research. There are three methodological types: survey, quasi-experiment and actual randomized experiment. The difference between these lies in the degree to which we can make general statements about a given population and the extent to which we can draw causal conclusions. Basically, this book offers a survey that identifies certain correlations between a variety of social factors.

1.2 To what extent can the respondents be seen as representative of the given population?

Surveys fall into two main types: probability sampling (simple random sampling) and non-probability sampling. The most typical form of the latter is quota sampling, where the sample taken is expected to reflect the basic constitution of a given population, such as age, sex and occupation, and our representative survey is based on quota sampling. Finally, the method of data collection needs to be identified. Three main techniques were employed: observation, self-reporting and hidden methods (such as measuring the delay in responses). During data collection based on self-reporting, respondents supply the data directly, through answering questions about their attitudes and opinions. It can be done with the help of interviews and questionnaires. For our study, we used only questionnaires. Our study is, therefore, a correlational social psychological survey, based on quota sampling through representative questionnaires. After the theoretical introduction, in each section, we first present the 2018 results and then correlate them with the 2010 survey.

1.3 The Rule of Law Report: Europe's view of Hungary

It remains necessary to situate our study in its immediate political context, which is a challenging task, since this context is mutable, especially in these times of international crisis. It is worth mentioning the 2019 European Commission's report on Rule of Law Report (the "Report"), which was published in September 2020, as part of its efforts to survey and present member states in the European Rule of Law Mechanism. The Report does not offer a positive image of Hungary, and the Commission expressed deep concern over a number of issues in relation to the rule of law. Naturally, the Commission's report did not survey the population's opinions, but rather considered shifts in the structure of the legal system that have taken place over recent years. Their way of assessing the situation in Hungary was, in other words, top-down, whereas our approach has been bottom-up. Yet, the population's pessimism regarding whether the judicial system was becoming more or less corrupt seems to have some basis, given the restructuring of the criminal justice system that has been going on behind the scenes.

In the first part, the Report reviews the Hungarian justice system and questions its full independence. It finds it worrying that the Chair of the National Council of the Judiciary (OBT) has too much responsibility in its central management of courts and finds it highly problematic that the members of the Hungarian Constitutional Court can, once they leave office, continue working as judges at the Kúria, Hungary's supreme court, without a standard appointment procedure, since the appointment of judges in the Constitutional Court requires the support of the legislative and the executive powers. Thus, the three "classical" branches of power meld because the Parliament and the government can, through their political preferences, influence the composition of the supposedly politically independent Kúria. As a consequence, the constitutional principle of the separation of the three branches of power does not prevail, though it is only fair to point out that the Report views the new systems and procedural solutions enacted within the past five years positively, so it would be too simplistic to conclude that there has been a straightforward power grab by the executive branch of government in recent years. Still, clearly, things are not quite as transparent as they should be.

The second part of the Report discusses corruption. It concludes that the rate of Hungarians who believe that corruption is a significant problem is higher than the European average, a finding that is wholly borne out by our statistics. This devastating view is echoed by numerous European Anti-Fraud Office (OLAF) reports, and the Rule of Law Report emphasizes that while several organizations prosecute corruption, statistics reveal that the Attorney General's Office does not do its task efficiently enough. In addition, the Report observes that despite the detailed regulations concerning declarations of wealth, related controls are limited and unsystematic. Furthermore, the National Anti-Corruption Strategy, as announced by the government for 2020–2022, does not extend to the several areas most frequently associated with corruption.

The third part of the Report dwells on media pluralism, and it is sharply critical of the governing party's influence over the selection of the members of the Media

Council of the National Media and Info-Communications Authority (NMHH), since the majority party in parliament can influence the composition of this prestigious committee. Furthermore, the Report observes that the "independent media" is subjected to systematic obstruction and intimidation, although this is not strictly a legal problem so much as a sociopolitical one.

Finally, the Report examines the system of checks and balances. It briefly outlines the details of the Emergency (in effect between 11 March 2020 and 18 June 2020) and some of the legislative developments that followed from this, but it does not take a position on this issue. It also investigates the work and the legal status of the Commissioner for Fundamental Rights. Statistical figures and legal regulations suggest that the ombudsman does not efficiently protect fundamental rights, such as freedom of expression, but at the same time, this fact does not mean that, in the words of the Report, "it does not make adequate efforts to protect all human rights".

Indeed, according to the Report, there is significant pressure on civil society and, citing another report, it claims that the current political power has launched a clear offensive against the civil sphere, curtailing the full exercise of human rights by both legal and practical means. However, these comments are not related to the system of checks and balances because instead of concerning themselves with the legal dimensions of state organizations, they focus on public affairs and events taking place within the sphere of the freedom of opinion. For the European Commission, the rule of law means that the same law is applicable to all members of society, including governments and parliamentary representatives. If the rule of law means this, then Hungary meets these criteria because, according to the law, all individuals, including political leaders and officials, are accountable if they violate norms. At the same time, it is important to mention that the Constitutional Court took the following position in its 11/1992. (III. 5.) AB ruling: "To declare that Hungary is governed by the rule of law is at once a factual statement and a program [for improvement]". Nearly 30 years after this ruling, the realization of this is still work in progress.

In addition to the numerous obligations that Hungary must fulfill due to its membership in the EU, a new system of state organizations has been established, new laws of procedure have been enacted and several important legal codes have been combined into new, twenty-first-century versions. It is, therefore, too simplistic to assert that Hungary's legal system is wholly corrupt, but it undoubtedly remains hamstrung by an inheritance of centralization and nepotism, which unscrupulous politicians and members of the judiciary could exploit to their full personal advantage.

Objectives

This book is the fourth cycle of a project launched in 2007. Its main objective is to get a better understanding of how the Hungarian population thinks about the law and of the changes that took place in these opinions between the spring of 2010 and the autumn of 2018. Our study hopes to contribute to the growing interest in legal consciousness and legal culture that the social sciences, especially sociology, social psychology, political science, criminology and legal sociology, have shown in recent years.

The 2018 phase of the project aimed to turn the 2010 national representative survey into a longitudinal study by collecting data using a very slightly modified questionnaire, which considers, in particular, the power of social media, and draws on a representative sample. From a theoretical perspective, our study registers changes in socio-demographic, psychological, social psychological factors and in opinions about crime, criminal justice and the prevention of crime by comparing data from 2010 and 2018. Beyond this, there is no further agenda. In other words, we do not attempt to provide interpretation or theorization of the changes, but essentially limit ourselves to the identification of "correlations" or "sociological patterns" that make further analyses and hypotheses possible. First, however, the study positions itself in the context of contemporary international (and Hungarian) legal sociology and criminology, so as to contribute to a broader understanding of the shifts in perception of civil society and the rule of law during Fidesz's ascendency.

2 Theoretical background

This chapter introduces and clarifies the basic concepts of the study of legal consciousness in legal sociology and other related empirical social sciences. This, in turn, enables our empirical results to be seen in the light of key areas of legal consciousness research, with which the reader may be unfamiliar, and to connect these two aspects of our study.[1] The final section in this chapter reviews related Hungarian studies from the past decade to assist in the interpretation of the local significance our findings.

2.1 The two levels of legal consciousness

Our study differentiates between the individual and the social levels of legal consciousness, a distinction that was established by "socialist legal sociology"[2] in the 1970s, in an obvious effort to comply with the tenets of the prevailing Marxist legal theory (and Marxist ideology generally). This compliance explains why the concept of the social, in distinction to the individual, remains ill-defined. Basically, although researchers knew full well that social hierarchies had remained firmly in place, the official views about the desirability of a classless society, together with the efforts to dissolve traditional communities and prevent new ones from spontaneously forming, worked against this recognition. As a result, many equated the social with the state. The individual was directly connected to the social sphere, without the mediation of class, religion or culture. Considering that the idea of legal pluralism – that multiple legal codes can coexist within one population – began to emerge in Anglo-American and Dutch legal anthropology several decades earlier,[3] Eastern Bloc legal theorists were fully aware of the overly simple nature of their model. Nonetheless, at this point of our study, we utilize this model, albeit with an awareness that we will later lay bare its contradictions. Figure 2.1 illustrates the interplay of two levels of legal consciousness.

Moving from society to the individual, we can isolate three fields at this early stage of the inquiry: socialization **(1a)**, communication **(1b)** and law enforcement **(1c)**. Looking at the flow from individual to society, one should separate the fields of communication **(1d)**, social actions with legal relevance **(1e)** and definite legal actions **(1f)**. On the social level, the institutional layer **(1g)** and social legal

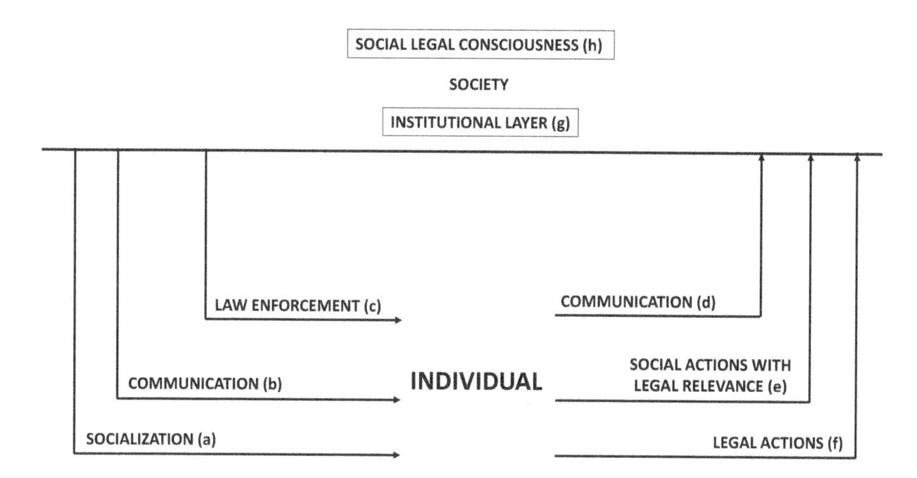

Figure 2.1 The individual and society

consciousness **(1h)** are to be distinguished. Each of these aspects is now going to be further defined and discussed in the context of our research.

1a. One caveat about our use of the term "socialization" is required: we use this term in a somewhat narrow sense, disregarding, for a moment, the fundamentally interactive nature of the learning process, the various ways in which the student exerts a particular influence on the teacher, which is not to demur from the Senecan adage: *homines dum docent discunt*. Still, we focus on the initial phase of social learning with its end point in young adulthood, even if researchers embracing the idea of lifelong learning rightly pay increasing attention to the concepts of resocialization and reeducation. The reason for this choice is that knowledge and experience associated with the law is accumulated and processed in the cognitive sphere of the personality, during legal socialization in adulthood, a fact highlighted in Figure 2.1, through the categories of social communication and law enforcement.

In the initial phases of identity formation, legal socialization does not differ significantly from other aspects of one's education, especially before puberty, when the various manifestations of rules and authority impact our personality though their emotive force. After puberty, however, the cognitive sphere becomes more decisive for personality development, and a gradual sophistication and enrichment of young people's knowledge of legal authority can be observed. This, in turn, leads to a more critical emotional and moral attitude toward the concept of the law. While the family is the primary factor in the early phases of socialization, later schools, the various peer groups and, increasingly, the media – especially, these days, the omnipresent social media – become formative influences.

Behind the attempts to understand and empirically explore socialization, there are two fundamental theoretical approaches. Based on the insights of Jean Piaget, the theory of "cognitive development"[4] was explicated by Lawrence Kohlberg and June L. Tapp in the 1970s,[5] whereas Ronald L. Akers and Albert Bandura posited the theory of "social learning" around the same time.[6] While the former puts emphasis on the inner dynamics of the cognitive development of the personality, the latter stresses the significance of external, social influences in their theoretical models of socialization. An integrated model of legal socialization was achieved by a combination of these approaches and was associated with the work of Ellen S. Cohn and Susan O. White in the 1980s.[7] Over the past half century, scholars of legal consciousness have identified a number of key concepts and practices in relation to the phenomenon of legal consciousness. These new developments, together with the empirical research that has been conducted in this field, have yielded important results[8]; preeminent among these is the conceptual separation of the cognitive elements of legal knowledge and legal reasoning from emotional motivation, evaluating attitudes and legal competence and employing theoretical knowledge to explain the internal structures of legal consciousness and the interactive dimensions of education.

1b. When looking at the direction of communication from society toward the individual, we need to note that we also maintain interest in the reverse of this flow; in other words, the feedback from the individual, a phenomenon discussed later. At this point, our focus is on the flow of information about the law as it is communicated by state institutions through various types of the media. This can include a wide range of information, beginning from the public announcement of an itemized list of legal regulations through the availability of court decisions to information about the workings of legislation and jurisdiction. Because this is usually indirect and unilateral communication, the usual problems can arise during the process: purposefully selected information or even manipulation or disinformation. To guarantee the rule of law and appropriate legal education, it is essential to counter these problems. One should not forget that the internal structures of, and the interplay between such media as the printed press, radio, motion pictures,[9] television, social media and the internet can significantly add to the complexity of this challenge. Indeed, social media platforms demand particular attention due to their impact on legal communication, not least because unlike other media, they communicate in an interactive way and create a kind of alternative publicity, which generally focuses on miscarriages of justice.[10]

One or another type of communication is inseparable from all other aspects of our study and social media, in particular, possesses significant agency. Another example is communication between parties during law enforcement or in situations where the expression of individual views becomes an issue, or in the cases of legal or legally relevant individual actions. It is due to the work of Jürgen Habermas,[11] Niklas Luhmann,[12] Günther Teubner[13] and Jacques Derrida[14] that communication achieved special importance in the social sciences of the 1960s–1980s. The 1990s saw David Nelken establish the field of "law as communication"[15] and make an effort to synthesize the European tradition of social sciences with those new trends in Anglo-American law studies that had been gaining traction since the 1980s, with special regard to fields such as "law and language",[16] "law and semiotics"[17] and "law and literature".[18] However, the related findings only exerted an impact on empirical legal sociology about a decade later and even then it was in methodological considerations rather than practical research.[19]

We collected, in all earlier phases of our study, data from the entire Hungarian population (including lawyers and law students) about diverse aspects of media consumption such as the credibility of certain types of media or the relationship between the printing press and the internet, and this large body of data has been used for surveying the general political orientation of the population. Its relevance for legal consciousness, however, has yet to be analyzed.

1c. Law enforcement corresponds to individual legal action **(1f)**, as shown in Figure 2.1. Traditionally, these two aspects cover the validation or realization of law. Thus, law enforcement means primarily the processes initiated *ex officio* by authorities, while individual law enforcement falls into the category of individual legal action. To put it simply, state jurisdiction, administration and criminal justice constitute the first category, while civil lawsuits and civil law jurisdiction represent the second. Furthermore, upon closer scrutiny, it becomes clear that the distinction between the two is not at all rigid in modern legal systems and mediation organizations exemplify this point.

According to a well-established doctrine, legal experience acquired during the course of law enforcement has a significant impact on individual legal knowledge and basic assumptions about the law. KOL-research in the 1990s confirmed this point.[20] Two theoretical approaches have emerged to clarify the influence of law enforcement on individual legal consciousness. One of them is associated with Richard Posner, who is a well-known representative of the field of law and economics.[21] As for its broader background, this approach relies on the theory of rational decisions and it is premised on the insight that efficient and calculable law enforcement makes compliance with the law "cheap", while violating or evading the law becomes "expensive". Another influential approach is associated with Tom R. Tyler:[22] the impact of law enforcement on individual legal consciousness is best captured through exploring earlier phases of socialization, when belief in the role of law is encouraged or, conversely, weakened. Whereas the discipline of law and economics focuses on the undesirable expenses associated with illegal behavior, the social psychological approach emphasizes the equitability of law enforcement, paying particular attention to fair play and procedural justice. Apart from this research inspired by the abovementioned two major theories, we should not ignore the efforts that arose mainly from legal anthropology, as it was cultivated, for example, by Sally Falk Moore[23] and Laura Nader[24] from the 1960s to the 1980s in the United States. These studies examine how legal experiences form around the process of law enforcement. In addition, they perform a micro-sociological analysis of law enforcement forums as "semi-autonomous social fields".

1d. Leaving aside the problematics of individual legal consciousness for a moment, we now face the challenge of understanding and explicating individual communication. As a first step, one should consider the differences between what people say, think and actually do. In other words, individual utterances about the law do not necessarily reflect what an individual actually thinks about the law and, more obviously, they can provide no guidance about how a person will act in a particular situation. Two important facts follow from this distinction.

First, we need to consider the political implications of individual legal communication. This is because articulating how one thinks about the law is inevitably a social act, one that carries, to a certain extent, elements of factual knowledge as well as the assessment of the law. Discoursing about the law assigns the individual a position in public opinion or, as Gabriel Almond and Sydney Verba would put it, one becomes part of an "upward"[25] move from citizens toward the government. Indeed, one contributes to the shaping of political culture. Thus, the connectedness of legal culture and political culture is apparent on the level of individual action.

All these considerations should make analysts more careful about their methodologies. It is not necessarily enough to study individual opinions, without studying the associated behavior. Hence, micro-sociological studies are of particular relevance in this field,[26] which is especially true when we consider the interactive nature of individual communication. Even the lowest levels of social discourse are defined by a variety of structural elements, including social layering, group formation, organizational forms and social fields, which need to be mapped. This, however, points beyond individual communication, the current phase of our model.

1e. When considering legally relevant individual social activities, we should distinguish between unlawful behavior and attempts to evade the law. Unlawful activities arise in a large variety, and it is especially true for the types of motivation behind them – a key field to be explored from the angle of legal consciousness. As one extreme, we could mention civil disobedience. It is a demonstrative, politically or morally motivated, open but non-violent refusal to comply with the law. Another extreme is when the law is violated out of sheer ignorance (*ignorantia iuris*). These acts might be the consequence of "alienation from the law", being carried away by emotions, or being misled; they may, in certain instances, be eminently justifiable too. There are many types of these, and their classification poses a challenge to those who study the concept of responsibility in various legal systems.

No comprehensive mid-level theory of non-compliance with the law has emerged in the international literature about legal consciousness.[27] Instead, KOL-research has explored this phenomenon in its relation to the earlier outlined theoretical directions (the various derivatives of social psychology or the theory of rational decisions) and with a view to existing responsibility systems in individual branches of the law. Given its moral and political weight, criminology plays the main role here and empirical studies in the area of non-compliance with civil law and state regulations receive much less attention.[28]

Evading the law reflects an individual's attempt to ignore the available legal means and resolve a conflict. Some of these possibilities include mediation and dispute resolution operating "in the shadow of the law"[29] and some function in more or less complete independence from state law. These latter ones operate on community or group levels, often presenting a peculiar mirror image of traditional procedures and informal social practices. Such forms of conflict resolution, which are regarded by many as just as reliable as state law mechanisms, have traditionally fallen within the scope of legal anthropology, but they moved from this field into legal sociology in the 1980s under the name of "informal justice" or "alternative dispute resolution"[30] and were complemented by studies in "restorative justice"[31] in the following decades. Serving as the direct foundation for the current research, the 2010 study probed both non-compliance with the law and evasion of the law. It helped us get a better estimate of the proportion of latent crime and understand the social perception of crime more accurately, while the later study helped us measure the degree of trust in law and justice – two questions on the survey inquired if the respondent believed it was a good idea at all to go to court.

1f. Legal activities can be divided into two components. One is the case of "passive" compliance with the law, which is when an individual simply meets legal regulations by all objective standards. The other case is when one resorts to the law consciously, which is when the law is a tool that serves an individual's interests. To study the rule and the efficacy of the law from a sociological perspective, the first component is more relevant, whereas to do the same from the perspective of legal consciousness, the second component is more significant. "Passive" compliance with the law involves meeting certain objective standards, and it is independent of the motivation for such behavior. Emphasis is placed on the fulfillment of the individual's legal obligations, which may have been established by certain authorities (e.g. to file a tax return in appropriate form and time), or arise between private individuals (thereby falling into the category of civil law). Following the scholarship of Eugen Ehrlich,[32] legal sociology recognizes the significance of having legal affairs resolved without a dispute (in the words of John Griffiths, these are "trouble-less cases")[33] for the entire legal system. This mass of legal action constitutes the "living law" even if we know that in reality "passive" compliance with the law should be attributed to other social norms, such as ethics, habits or manners.

This type of legal action is quite different from the one where the law is a tool for the individual. In this situation, not only is a relatively sophisticated knowledge of the law, but also a particular attitude is required,[34] as is a sense of entitlement. This means that the individual approaches the authorities not from the position of begging, but from that of claiming.[35] However, this is not merely a matter of personal background and attitude; to use the law as a tool necessarily involves the existence of certain external conditions, most obviously, time and money, and, without these, one cannot be expected to start a lawsuit. Because the distribution of these sources is quite uneven in society, legal sociology has been exploring this phenomenon as the theme of "access to law" since the 1980s.[36] To study the first type of legal activity (also known as the "living law") requires micro-sociological, legal anthropological and qualitative (document analysis oriented) research. To study the second type, the sense of entitlement, the readiness to go to court and the civil litigation rate should be mapped.[37] As previously mentioned in connection with law evasion, an earlier stage in our study contained a poll that surveyed the degree of trust people had in courts. The decline in public faith in the legal system that this book pinpoints between 2010 and 2018 clearly correlates with an increase in overt criminality and a more "flexible" attitude toward passive compliance, such as completing tax returns.

1g. Following the upward move from individual to society, we reach again the "social level", which, in more traditional terms, is identical with the levels of state or governmental organizations. But some caution is required here. On the one hand, the word "state" or "governmental" connotes the dominance of the political, even if our study focuses on the significance of the legal dimension. It is from this perspective that Lawrence Friedman identifies this institutional layer – besides legal norms and legal culture – as one element of the legal system.[38] Similarly relevant is Blankenburg's notion of "legal infrastructure",[39] which includes, in certain situations, the various non-state organizations that can institutionalize evasion of the law.

On the other hand, the standard terminology does not reflect adequately on organizational complexity. What we have in mind is not limited to the functional separation of legislation, law enforcement and regulatory authorities in their reproduction of the political doctrine of the separation of powers. In reality, legal institutions have extremely complex inner divisions by reference to their organizational interests, their relation to power and communication, and their access to social resources. Needless to say, a number of related factors impact general trust in legal systems, including the mass of individual, positive and negative experiences or the ideal image of the law as shaped by socialization and social communication. Among these factors, one finds such issues as the coordinated and transparent structure of legal institutions, their efficient and reliable operations, easy access to them, their availability for public and democratic supervision and, finally, the general ethos of these organizations (Does the state serves its citizens, or is it the other way round?).[40] The 2010 stage of our study surveyed the degree of trust people had in courts. In addition, two further questions surveyed the general assessment of Hungarian society and attitudes toward legislation and law enforcement. This data may help theorists of legal consciousness to get a clearer, more accurate idea about the relationship between citizens and state or governmental institutions. What arises from this is that people increasingly conceive of themselves as subjects of the state rather than empowered citizens.

1h. At this point, we advocate a quite radical correction in relation to the concept of "social legal consciousness". As we mentioned at the beginning of this section, the term appeared in the "Marxist legal sociology" in the 1970s, but it is still present in the contemporary socio-legal studies. Mainly among the representatives influenced by the *Critical Legal Studies* movement who apply the term "legal consciousness" to ideological structures as detectable on individual, group, class and social levels.

Yet, we believe that the appropriate term to use is not "legal consciousness" but "legal culture". It appears to be both clearer and more operational from the perspective of legal sociology. First of all, we need to realize that there is a difference between how legal consciousness on a social level connects with the institutional sphere, which represents the political community as a whole and is customarily identified with the state or the government, and how individual legal consciousness connects with the individual as a psycho-physical reality. Unlike in the relationship of individual and individual legal consciousness, the state is definitely not the one and only formative element behind social legal consciousness. While it is theoretically possible to reconstruct individual legal consciousness from their behavior, the activities of state organizations do not permit us to form an accurate image of social legal consciousness because this latter concept carries complex meanings that cannot be reduced to or identified with the domain of the state.

The most obvious argument in favor of our suggestion, which, nevertheless, has far reaching methodological implications, is that the concept of "social legal consciousness" assumes the existence of some "collective personality", which is similar to the Marxist concept of "class consciousness", but this idea of a collective personality just does not make sense from the empirical perspective, while in a narrow psychological sense, only an individual can have consciousness and everything that is at once external, objective and yet intangible can be described as culture.

This change in terminology, however, does not eliminate all theoretical difficulties. Consider, for example, the controversy about Lawrence M. Friedman's notion of legal culture,[41] against which Roger Cotterrell formulated quite powerful counterarguments.[42] First, legal culture is merely a residual category when viewed from the perspective of sociological studies; second, it is used in a too comprehensive way; and third, Friedman's distinction between "external" and "internal" legal culture is unclear. For our present purposes, the concept of legal culture is defined as a set of values, norms, symbols, narratives and patterns of social practices. Legal culture is related to political culture through the concept of legitimacy, and it is organically woven into the texture of the entire culture. Indeed, a political and social culture's legitimacy is in no small way contingent upon the independence and reliability of its legal system.

2.2 Individual and society: how do we think about the law?

John Griffiths' criticism on the instrumental approach to law is a promising opening for our argument.[43] He advises his readers not to forget that the individual is never connected directly to the state; instead, it is always a set of, often overlapping, groups and communities that connect the two. He also points out that a legal message from the law maker never reaches the addressee through some sort of normative vacuum and that the state does not have a normative monopoly. With these warnings in mind, we can now start reviewing the structures that stand between the individual and the state, as shown in Figure 2.2.

2a. The "hard facts" that define an individual's social status include one's gender, age, wealth, income, education and place of residence. The ways in which these impact legal knowledge and legal consciousness were first explored in the KOL-research of the 1960s as carried out by Adam Podgóreczky and his colleagues.[44] The findings showed that all the abovementioned factors had some impact on one's legal consciousness, but no general pattern or correlation emerged. It seemed that although minor patterns could be identified, these varied from country to country, from one legal culture to another. Two tendencies can be identified in later discussions of this: the first is that education impacts legal consciousness

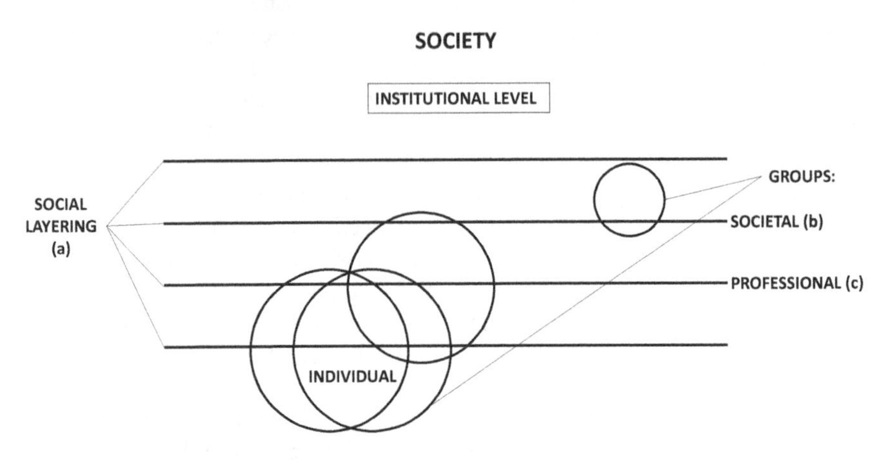

Figure 2.2 Social layering and the individual

most significantly, whereas the other suggests that gender differences in relation to one's legal knowledge and general attitude toward the law diminish over time. Hungarian legal consciousness research has always paid extensive attention to the issue of social layering, and the related longitudinal studies in legal knowledge and legal consciousness also confirmed the existence of these tendencies.[45] Likewise, the 2010 questionnaire explored the social class of respondents. We recorded data such as place of residence, gender, age, education, marital status, occupation, financial status by objective (income per capita in one household) and subjective standards. The analysis of the data revealed that the Hungarian population is very divided in regard to their general attitude toward the law, with wealthier respondents having a greater faith in the rule of law than poorer ones, a divide that increased during the period studied (2010–2018).

2b. Groups defined by family, ethnicity, locality, age, religion and worldview[46] are the most significant units among societal groups. Owing to the strong psychological impact of direct, face-to-face communication, societal groups can shape the individual's identity powerfully. Even if scholars always assumed that societal groups exert major influence on individual legal consciousness, actual research did not begin until the mid-1970s, when the method of participatory observation was borrowed from anthropologists. During the following decades, scholars could study the formation of individual attitudes toward, and assumptions about, the law in such varied environments as Israeli kibbutzim,[47] Central-American Chiapas communities[48] and US suburbia.[49]

2c. Groups of professionals constitute in fact the social structure that is based on the division of labor, including all institutions and organizations, operating within the spheres of economy, politics, culture and, of course, the law. The affiliation between the individual and a group of professionals – or one's "occupation" – is in itself a component of one's social status, although this component has lost some of its significance over the past decades. Nevertheless, the presence and participation in certain professional groups or orders, such as companies, trade unions or political parties, definitely impact the participant's legal knowledge and legal consciousness, in that doing their jobs makes the acquisition of certain legal skills and experience necessary.

In the first phase of KOL-research, studies focus on legal attitudes by reference to occupational status.[50] From the 1980s onward, however, both international[51] and Hungarian[52] research began to focus only on lawyers as a professional group. The law is a high-prestige career, with most participants emerging from a middle-class background. Law students receive a special training and earn a degree, which is then followed by practical training. The professional order of lawyers can be broken down into professional groups (e.g. judges, barristers, prosecutors), along structural principles that vary from country to country, from legal culture to legal culture. A number of factors affect the cohesion between various members of this order, the self-image that these professionals have, and also the image that society has about its lawyers. These factors include, for example, the internal structure of this professional order, the implications of this structure for the prestige that professional groups possess, and also the various patterns of mobility that the structure permits. Evidently, lawyers are characterized by a much higher degree of legal knowledge and legal competence than lay people. However, it does not necessarily mean that they are more law abiding than lay members of the society.

Indeed, the social function and the monopoly of lawyers is to create and maintain the normative layer of legal culture and to cultivate the associated doctrinal-dogmatic layer. In this regard, it is useful to revisit the definition of legal culture (2.1. Item If). Just as Friedman distinguished between "external" and "internal" legal culture,[53] we recommend now the separation of "lay" and "professional" legal cultures. It is obvious that the former has greater relevance for the formation of legal culture as a whole. The significant difference between lay ideas about the law in general and the professionals' notion of the law is that they communicate it internally among their own ranks and externally.

Finally, two more comments should be added to this outline of the mediating structures between individuals and society. First, we focused on corporative groups and on structural elements that can be distinguished clearly from society as a whole and we ignored the so-called "semi-autonomous social fields". These are fields of force in which both individuals and corporative groups can appear with the capability to create and maintain an independent system of norms. The only way to approach these subtle components of social structure is through a micro-sociological methodology, such as the one adopted in this book. Second, the thoroughly interrelated effects of mediating structures multiply and intensify the workings of legal socialization, communication and activities. It also means that the possible objects of related research can multiply. Small wonder, then, that ordinary people with no legal or academic background find it extremely difficult to gain a comprehensive idea about how the law works.

2.3 Legal culture

As a preliminary formulation of the concept, we have defined *legal culture* as the sum of various idiosyncratic patterns of values, norms, symbols, social practices, cultural descriptions and narratives associated with the law. Through the concept of legitimacy, legal culture is closely linked to political culture and to culture in general, and no clear boundaries can be drawn. Furthermore, we divided the sphere of "lay" and "professional" culture within the realm of legal culture. The "professional legal culture" evidently has the determining importance in the formation of legal culture as a whole. Although it is also clear that the "lay culture" – that is the vision of law in the sight of non-lawyers – can be utterly different from the picture lawyers would like to project inward (toward other lawyers) and outward (toward the external social environment). To demonstrate the concept of legal culture, let us present an analysis of a constituent of professional legal culture, the attorneys' professional self-image, used in a recent empirical study.[54] Self-image is essentially a cultural phenomenon, differing from social psychological processes that determine its motifs and, therefore, influence individual or group behavior. Consequently, the discourse about attorneys' self-image must be placed into the one about legal culture. In this sense, the self-image of the attorney's profession is viewed as one of the elements of professional legal culture as opposed to lay citizens' legal culture. The self-image of the profession, however, can be interpreted as an ensemble of intellectual elements and content, a tapestry of values, norms, prescriptive cultural patterns, narratives and symbols; and the sociological patterns can be read out from the conduct of the representatives of the profession.

Values characteristic of the self-image of the attorney's profession, such as professional preparedness (a high level of legal knowledge), a sense of justice, impartiality and the unconditional respect for the interests of the client, belong to the more general values of the broader legal profession and are embedded in the even more comprehensive values of political culture such as liberty, equality and social solidarity. One of the layers of self-image is found closer to the level of social activities and comprises the rules of the profession. Part of these rules are "written", such as the binding rules of Act No. XI of 1998 on attorneys or other rules of legal nature such as the codes of conduct of the Hungarian Bar Association (hereafter the Bar). The profession has unwritten rules as well, including the "courtesy" rules on the interactions with colleagues or lay citizens, which also form part the profession's self-image.

Descriptive cultural patterns do not prescribe what ought to be done in a particular situation, but they set out the positions and competences of the participants. They also designate the place and the scope of activities that take place within the society or in the legal sphere. In this case, it can be interpreted to include the rules on pleas and trial organization laid down in the act on civil procedure the recipients of which are primarily judges. They also set forth attorneys' positions and their options to influence the course of an ongoing trial.

The values and the layers of prescriptive and descriptive cultural patterns analytically separated are, in this case, entwined by narratives, stories known and narrated by attorneys. They also create the "normative universe" coined by Robert Cover, in which these patterns acquire their meaning.[55] Every profession has its "great stories", such as the development of the Hungarian attorney's profession, which is elaborated on and lectured about at universities to future attorneys within the discipline of legal history. These narratives are coiled around major turning points and outstanding figures of the profession as a corporate group and form the basis of the entire professional group. The fabric of local "urban legends" and personal stories, which inherently relate to other cultural fields, are also woven into these narratives.[56]

Symbols expressing self-image are not to be construed as physical realities, such as luxury cars, expensive watches, powdered wigs, gowns, the latest mobile phones or state-of-the-art laptops. Rather, they are to be interpreted as signs with multiple meanings. Symbols can signal the fact of belonging to the in-group and, at the same time, they are able to animate complex emotions and knowledge content in outsiders. As for attorneys, status symbols bear a major significance, which not only signal their belonging to the middle class but also create an impression of success with clients, such as the luxury car or the expensive watch. However, other symbols (such as an attorney's briefcases) signal their owner's profession. One must also mention the pattern layers inferred from the behavior of those practicing the profession, which are grouped under *tacit* knowledge and which are acquired by professionals entering the profession through observation of their colleagues' not-so-obvious activities. These are the tricks of the trade, which can only be mastered by practicing and which are more often than not markedly different from the idealized values and rules of the profession's manifest self-image.

It is important to note here that contradictions and internal tensions generally arise among the elements of self-image, despite the basic tendency to strive for intellectual unity and internal coherence during the formation of the professional self-image. Presumably, the more coherent and clear the self-image is, the more it can ensure cohesion among those practicing the profession, which may contribute to the assertion of interests within professional circles. Conversely, the more contradictory, fragmented and vague the self-image of the profession is, the less it will be able to integrate its members and the more vulnerable it will become in the face of adversities. The role of a solid and clear professional self-image from the point of view of how it has evolved socially is always an empirical question: an overly strong corporate spirit may also become a hindrance to reacting adequately to social change.

Finally, one must acknowledge the dynamic relation between the self-image of the profession and the image created of the profession by lay citizens. In conclusion, the structure of lay legal culture is similar to the professional, although its normative layer is much thinner and it is rather more fragmented and loaded with more logical contradictions. The presence of these two characteristics, relatively low level of knowledge[57] and the existence of logical contradictions, was detected,[58] in particular, by our 2018 legal sociological studies of the Hungarian population, the majority of whom seem unaware what exactly it is that lawyers do and what the symbols of their profession mean.

2.4 Individual legal consciousness

To relate our study to traditional notions about the structure of the individual psyche, we should first review the key categories through which studies in the 1970s approached individual legal consciousness: legal consciousness and legal knowledge. Of the two, legal consciousness is the more comprehensive concept. Legal knowledge is one of its constituents through its connectedness to the cognitive (conscious and rational) sphere of the individual psyche. To a certain extent, legal consciousness is a residual category because it covers all the psychological moments that are not parts of legal knowledge, such as the affective (emotions or the unconscious) or reactive workings of the psyche. Let us then review the rational (a), emotional (b) and volitional (c) components of legal consciousness and then the structure of legal consciousness (d).

Item a. In this context, the concept of legal knowledge calls for a broader definition than just familiarity with the rules of positive law, because comprehending the law and using it as a tool assumes a certain degree of familiarity with the dogmatic layer. KOL-research has already made it clear that legal knowledge in itself is neither a necessary nor a sufficient condition of compliance with the law, even if legal knowledge is an inevitable element of legal competence.[59] Empirical studies have revealed that lay people's legal knowledge is quite limited,[60] limited enough to take the principle of *ignorantia juris non excusat* seriously. In addition, this knowledge varies from legal field to legal field. As a rule, penal law is best known, while civil law and public administration are more obscure terrains, perhaps for reasons that have to do with the historical obscurification of these areas under socialism. Likewise, lay people know more about substantive law than about procedural rules. Education and legal experience are the two most important factors in generating knowledge, whereas differences in age, gender, income or media consumption matter significantly less.[61]

Of course, the concept of legal knowledge does not subsume everything associated with the law in the cognitive sphere, in that the prejudices and preconceptions that may affect a given legal decision clearly belong here. They are, in fact, an integral part of KOL-research. It is necessary, in this respect, to pose the general philosophical question: to what extent does rationality govern individual action? It is generally assumed in the modern legal doctrine that human beings are capable of understanding the law, acting in harmony with the law and considering the consequences of their actions rationally; the theory of rational decisions is quite close to this view, while social psychological approaches argue that people comply with the law much more frequently than the times when rational calculations would make it worthwhile for them.[62]

Item b. Discussing legal behavior from the perspective of emotions raises the following question: do human have some sort of innate sense of justice or legality?

The legal tradition answers this question positively; for example, late nineteenth-century law scholars Herman Post and Joseph Kohler, founders of German ethnological legal studies, find it evident that a sense of justice (*Rechtsgefühl*) is a core component of the human mind. This was the reason why they promoted the idea of a universal law that is not dependent on historical and social circumstances.[63] This view lost much of its appeal in the second half of the twentieth century when the theory of instinct reduction[64] came into ascendency and denied the existence of an instinct responsible for one's sense of justice. However, this problematic can be reconsidered in the light of Konrad Lorenz's research in the 1970s.[65]

Next, we should ask how related concepts such as "loyalty", "respect", "trust", or "fear" and "anxiety" can be situated in the context of law, especially given that motivation is principally emotional rather than rational. The related theoretical and sociological studies have increasingly relied on the recent insights of neuroscience. In fact, a new, independent field of interdisciplinary research called "law and emotions" seems to be arising. The studies of András Sajó are particularly relevant in this context, and they detail how, through a reciprocal dynamic between private moral feelings and legal/political institutions, the phenomenon of legal (constitutional) public sentiment arises.[66]

Item c. Traditional legal scholarship tended to classify non-compliance with the law as a volitional problem. When discussing volition in a psychological context, a key issue is the issue of "forcefulness". Legal competence entails not only legal knowledge but also readiness for conflict. Hungarian legal consciousness research in the 1970s seems to support this thesis. The analysts used a Personal Frustration Tolerance test to establish a link between personal frustration tolerance and deviant behavior tolerance. The findings revealed that individuals with a higher frustration tolerance level are invariably less tolerant toward deviant behavior.[67] It is also often experienced that aging people are less ready to be engaged in conflicts that their will power "softens". In this context, we should note a recent development in the theory of rational decisions, which helps analyze the problem of weakening will ("the Odysseus-problem").[68] This leads us to the next, more general question: how do emotions and rationality affect intentions? Ultimately, it seems that research in legal consciousness has yet to incorporate the findings of related scientific research.

Item d. To explore the structure of individual legal consciousness, we need to address a particular phenomenon, in which separate elements of the consciousness (rationality, emotions, volition) are integrated in much the same way as narratives unify disparate cultural elements (values, norms and symbols) within a given legal culture. Thus, attitudes integrate cognitive, emotive and reactive moments. According to Gordon W. Allport's classic definition, attitude is acquired through experience and it indicates a mental state of readiness.[69]

Once the first phases of KOL-research had been completed, analysts recognized that individual legal consciousness does not produce a coherent, unified set of ideas about the law. Subsequent international[70] and Hungarian studies[71] also highlighted the fragmented nature of individual legal consciousness. We should view individual legal consciousness as fragmented, a field of numerous internal contradictions, which prevent the rise of a coherent dimension of consciousness. For this reason, attitudes about the law are, to a great extent, dependent on various social contexts. However, we should not forget that even in its fragmented state, the structures of individual legal consciousness combine into patterns on group or social levels, lending themselves to sociological interpretation and that exploring these patterns leads to a comparative study of legal cultures and histories.

2.5 Individual legal consciousness and legal culture: the social psychological aspect

In essence, this book aims to capture the relationship between culture and individual consciousness through exploring the psychological patterns and mechanisms of individual and social interactions. The present project relies on the same theory of "social representations" that we introduced in detail in our 2010 volume. This approach concentrates on the process where previously unknown content (objects, ideas) becomes the elements of daily cultural life, after moving through various channels of social communication in a given community.

Such research involves studying multiple layers of culture, including individual attitudes, stereotypes, prejudices, channels of social communication, beliefs and assumptions, the ways in which these assumptions create social patterns, the symbols and narratives that help them find integration into other narratives or larger cultural patterns. Supplementary disciplines such as semiotics or pragmatics can be helpful. Our questionnaire-based method continues the methodology of our 2010 study. Its focus is on prejudices, attitudes and personality traits, the patterns that these elements form and the relationship between them. Thus, the questionnaire for the 2010 data collection includes several queries about beliefs, evaluating attitudes and stereotypes, which are detailed in the next chapter. Because the questionnaire explored attitudes about the law and politics, it could also be used as a starting point of analyses of political psychology.[72]

At this point, let us return to the concepts of legal culture and social legal consciousness. In our earlier discussion, we suggested discarding the latter category. Correspondingly, when we were listing the elements of legal culture, we left out attitudes because these were carried by individual members of society and, therefore, attitudes belong to the level of individual legal consciousness. Considering, however, how significant social psychological perspectives are for empirical studies and how unevenly individual attitudes appear in larger social contexts, interpreting legal consciousness on a social level is a legitimate possibility. After all, this idea appears in Kahei Rokumoto's 2004 work,[73] in which the author considers legal culture as part of social legal consciousness, coexisting with legal knowledge, legal attitudes and legal sentiments. The core element of legal culture is legal conception, which is a permanent category, unlike legal knowledge or legal attitudes, which are volatile, even within a short period.[74] Because we decided, after careful deliberation, to discard the notion of "social legal consciousness", it would be misguided to bring it back as some sort of residual category in order to simply accommodate all those social psychological elements (such as attitudes, opinions, beliefs, mass emotions) that cannot be unambiguously seen as constituents of the concept of legal culture. To proceed, let us review two possible theoretical directions as outlined in Marc Hertogh's valuable recent article on legal consciousness.

Hertogh distinguishes between two strategies in his discussion of the structure of the concept of legal consciousness: the US and the European approaches.[75] The first one is based on the contributions of Roscoe Pound, and its key insight is the distinction between "Law in Books and Law in Action".[76] Legal sociology research aims to explore the difference between these two. In other words, it is interested in how, and to what extent, law in practice diverges from law in its official form. In their awareness of this difference, legal consciousness studies investigate people's perspective on official law. Law then becomes an independent variable, and legal consciousness a factor to explain deviation from the law.

The European concept of legal consciousness, however, has been inspired mainly by the scholarship of Eugen Ehrlich,[77] with the idea of "living law" at its center. Thus, sociological research should focus not on official law, but on the actual center of legal life, that is, the living law. This is because state organizations only rely on official law to decide legal cases, but the living law prevails in cases that complete themselves without a debate, a situation that characterizes most legal affairs. From this perspective, the question is not so much how people perceive the official law, but what it is that they perceive as law at all. The law becomes a dependent variable in this context.

Hertogh also makes a distinction between critical and secular approaches to legal consciousness.[78] The first one is closely connected to Critical Legal Studies, with its significant neo-Marxist inspiration, and also to the American concept of legal consciousness, as outlined earlier. This approach has defined several important publications during the final three decades of the twentieth century.[79] These studies explored the hegemony and ubiquitous presence of the law and attempted to answer the question why people keep turning to the law even if it regularly disappoints them. In short, the acceptance of, and support for, the law interested the authors of these works. In contrast to this, the secular approach,[80] as represented by Hertogh himself, refuses to see the hegemony of the law as a given through relying on the European concept of legal consciousness. It concentrates mainly on the reasons why people do not insist on the official version of the law and what sort of alternatives they seek. Instead of studying the acceptance of the law, this approach focuses on alienation from the law, evasion of the law, opposition to the law and those forms of alternative social control that often replaces official law.

What conclusions can we draw from this? First, we need to perceive legal social consciousness as a phenomenon closely connected to legal culture in general. From the perspective of legal consciousness, the law (legal culture) sometimes appears as an independent variable and sometimes as a dependent one. Legal culture shapes legal consciousness and, at the same time, it is shaped by legal consciousness. In fact, we need to envision the US and the European concepts of legal consciousness in Hertogh's model as two sides of the same coin, with permanent interplay between them. Second, we should approach legal consciousness as a field with its inner divisions. In this structure, the individual is connected to society through societal and professional groups, just like legal culture itself is a divided field. Furthermore, it is far from certain that the official law can fully prevail in all segments of society. For this reason, studying negative attitudes and emotions toward the law is just as important as investigating the acceptance of and support for the law.

2.6 Individual legal consciousness, social legal consciousness and legal culture

Considering how difficult it is to separate individual legal consciousness and social legal consciousness and how deeply the idea of social legal consciousness is embedded into traditions of Marxist thought from where such undesirable associations as "class consciousness" or "collective personality" may arise, we discarded the notion of social legal consciousness at the beginning of our study. Instead, we have chosen to use the concept of legal culture and to place all phenomena of a psychological nature into the category of individual legal consciousness. As a first step, we have defined *legal culture* as the sum of various idiosyncratic patterns of values, norms, symbols and social practices associated with the law. In the next phase of our discussion, we introduced the distinction between "lay" and "professional" legal cultures and elaborated on the internal structure of legal culture.

However, we realized during this process that our concept of legal culture was somewhat incomplete and inconsistent. Therefore, we decided to revisit our decision to discard the notion of social legal consciousness in the final section of our study. After careful deliberation, we chose to reintroduce the concept of social legal consciousness and, in a clear break from the Marxist origins of the term, to reinterpret it through its connectedness with legal culture. In this phase of our work, we relied on the work of Kahei Rokumoto and Marc Hertogh.

The question remains, however, what are then the key features of this new theoretical construct that we have recreated multiple times to facilitate our legal consciousness research? First, we need to see that modulations within legal consciousness take place in structures with multiple levels and layers and with permanent interplay between these levels. A complex tissue of legal knowledge, volitional and emotional elements, and individual legal consciousness organizes itself in accordance with the psychology of individuals. However, social legal consciousness, which is the sum of all manifestations of individual legal consciousness and has, therefore, only limited independence, is governed by the inner dynamics of social interactions. In addition, social legal consciousness is inseparably connected to legal culture, a sphere that fixates forms and objectified intellectual contents that are more permanent than mass emotions and public opinion, but at the same time, it is itself subject to changes. When these changes reach a certain intensity and affect social structure, it leads to transformations within social legal consciousness. Second, it should be noted that individual legal consciousness, social legal consciousness and legal culture with its internal division conform to social structure, that system of structural elements within which the individual is linked to the whole of society. Therefore, studies in legal consciousness are inseparable from studies in legal institutions, legal infrastructure and those formal and informal organizations and fields of force where competing forms of social control operate.

2.7 Our study in the context of contemporary international and Hungarian empirical research

To briefly review social studies with relevance for legal consciousness research, we focus on the empirical studies that were conducted between 2010 and 2018 and review only the type of research that connects thematically with ours. For example, we do not review the most recent research in the legal consciousness of law students, but our fields of interest include (a) legal sociology, (b) criminology, (c) social psychology and (d) political sociology.

In Hungary, three major studies in legal consciousness were conducted after 2010. The first study was conducted by Róbert Richard Kiss and Ágnes Zsidai in 2013.[81] Kiss and Zsidai collected data from a nearly representative sample (n = 973), using a questionnaire with sixty-five questions. The themes examined included numerous aspects of legal consciousness, such as the general nature of law, the relationship between the state and the law, legal certainty, assumptions about state institutions (separately examining courts, self-governments, the tax authorities and, as yet another category, prosecutors and attorneys), legal knowledge to resolve conflicts and legal sense. We found that some of the items belonging to themes such as "the general nature of law" and "the relationship between the state and the law" are just too embedded from a cognitive perspective, reflecting theoretical considerations rather than ordinary thought. It must be added that we saw interesting questioning techniques too, for example, when attitudes about the death penalty are examined together with legal knowledge about it. The main weakness of the study is the lack of sociometric analysis. We only have the basic distribution of the answers, in a non-convertible SPSS file rendering subsequent statistical analysis not necessarily impossible, but quite difficult. Next we should mention the study conducted by Zoltán Fleck. From a methodological point of view, this research has outstanding significance. It offered us the contents-based analysis of life story interviews. This qualitative method relies on the theory of social representations and narrative psychology, just like our present project, although our focus is essentially empirical.

All of the forty interviews were recorded between September 2014 and May 2015. The researchers arranged the findings of their survey in three thematic blocks in a volume, such as "historical context and identity", "vulnerable identities" and "legal consciousness and behavior at workplaces".[82] Whereas the study as a whole did not fully meet the researchers' expectations, it has nevertheless contributed to a better understanding of how striving for narrative coherence works. It also illuminates why "ordinary people" feel alienated from, and distrustful toward, the law.

It is, however, the study conducted by György Gajduschek between 2012 and 2019 that is the most closely connected to our project. Data was collected in several phases and in a methodologically varied manner. The first, the so-called "omnibus survey", used a representative sample, and it collected data about legal knowledge. Then, using again a representative sample, a questionnaire explored various aspects of legal consciousness. This material was supplemented by focus group interviews in the last phase of the project and also by data from a Serbian and Dutch representative sample and from the databases of *European Social Survey* and *Eurobarometer*. These supplementary elements were used to make a comparative study of entitlement culture possible. In time, we hope to survey other legal cultures in the region in order to enable comparable comparative analyses. Several analyses of Gajduschek's rich empirical material have so far been published and more are yet to come, so let us now review the main findings of these publications.

György Gajduschek and Balázs Fekete conducted a longitudinal study using the data that was collected during Kálmán Kulcsár's 1965 research into legal knowledge. The analysis required the correction or reconsideration of a number of factors: the no longer existing socialist structure, outdated legal regulations and certain distortions during the data collection all needed to be reviewed. The comparative analyses clearly indicate a significant increase in legal knowledge (about 35%), even if the larger context for this is the generally improving educational background of the overall population over the past half century (the significantly higher number of college and university students is particularly responsible for this). Apart from this tendency, it is only the much better knowledge of constitutional law that we can link to the social-political changes starting in 1989. To answer the question what defines the level of legal knowledge, the only source of data was from 2013. Today, we can safely claim that educational background is by far the most decisive factor.[83]

István Szilágyi and Gajduschek's work studies the correlation between educational principles and the readiness to inflict punishment. They sought answers to three questions. Do educational principals really affect the punitive inclination? What kind of changes can be observed in social expectations concerning applicable penalties since the mid-1980s? In a European context, what does the readiness to punish reflect? As to the first question, it is true that educational principles within the family impact how ready a person is to inflict punishment on others. But at the same time, analyzing the data signals that there is no obvious correlation between higher degree of punitivity and authoritarian, "traditional" or disciplinary behavioral models within the family. Thus, educational principles shape penalty expectations, but they do not explain them in themselves because these expectations remained high even though educational principles have changed during the examined period. This is also an indirect answer to the second question. Hardly any changes can be observed in penalty expectation of the Hungarians in comparison to earlier decades. As to the level of these expectations, the findings suggest that this is unusually high, about two times higher than the European average.[84] This book is particularly important for us because we transferred the question about death penalty into the questionnaire that we used for this book. As a result, a larger database is now available for further analyses.

Using James L. Gibson and Gregory A. Caldeira's 1996 publication,[85] Fekete and Péter Róbert examined Hungarian legal attitudes in an international context. Gibson and Caldeira relied on a study conducted by *Eurobarometer* and attempted to capture the general character of Western European legal attitudes in the member states of the then European Economic Community, exploring the rule of law, the neutrality of the law and the question of individual freedom. The Hungarian analysts collected data from a representative sample of the Hungarian population in 2015, which showed that the most adequate understanding of domestic legal attitudes is possible through a four-factor structure. Thus, the study revealed that Hungarians have a stronger need for predictability and paternalism than West-Europeans and that they value individual freedom less, which is perhaps unsurprising given the country's history. These differences have an impact on how legal values are structured. All in all, however, the findings did not demonstrate significant differences from the West-European situation.[86]

Zsolt Boda's study relies on Tom R. Tyler's theory (see 2.1. Item 1c.) and aims to clarify the relationship between trust, legitimacy and compliance with the law. Later, he refers to data in *European Social Survey* and demonstrates the fluctuations of trust in institutions (including the legal system, the police, the parliament, politicians and political parties) and between individuals. He covered the period from 2002 to 2012. One of the interesting findings is that more trust in the police than in courts can be detected. The database also made an international comparison possible. This revealed that trust in institutions is weaker in the East than in the West, in fact, the further east one goes, the weaker it is. Trust seems to be closely related to certain macro-level variables, such income per capita or the general level of trust. Hungarian data follows this trend; however, trust in institutions is slightly stronger than in other countries in the same region. For these reasons, the study concludes that one should not necessarily subscribe to the concept that appears in the late 1980s and claims that trust in the Hungarian legal system is critically low.[87]

Similarly, Gajduschek's study in 2013 examined trust in legal institutions and compliance with the law. Pollsters asked a smaller pool of people about their motivation in complying with the prohibition of smoking at bus stops. There were five possible answers, and most respondents claimed it was the fear of a fine that motivated them. The study not only offered a detailed statistical analysis, but it also formulated an interesting critique of Tyler's theory. According to this critique, in a social situation where people have only limited trust in the legal system and feel alienated from the law instead, the first step to restore the reliability of the legal system is the consistent application of fines and other sanctions.[88]

Róbert and Fekete explored a particular aspect of trust in institutions, which is "trust in lawsuits". If people assume they are right, how do they see their chances? The 2015 analysis focused on a representative sample of the Hungarian population, where the respondents were asked about their chances in seven imaginary situations where they sue their neighbors, their boss, a bank, the police, the tax authority, a wealthy entrepreneur and a politician. Analyzing the data revealed that the answers depended on, among other factors, educational background, level of income, place of residence, religion, general satisfaction and trust in institutions. According to the analysts, these correlations highlight basic cultural facts (the lack of the so-called "rights culture") and historical facts (skepticism about the legitimacy of the state and traditional state support of authoritarian regimes).[89] Szilágyi conducted a study in 2015 where he relied on data collected from focus groups and where he explored the kind of ethos that justifies the violation of social norms in everyday situations and in the related interpersonal communications. The most recent analysis was carried out by Gajduschek who, in cooperation with András Jakab, studied the lack of "entitlement culture" and the alienation from the law in the Hungarian population through a comparison with Serbian and Dutch data.[90]

As we suggested earlier, our research is closely connected to victimology, an important field of criminology. Among other tasks, victimology studies latent crime, the fear of crime, and opinions about and attitudes toward crime and crime rate. In this respect, we need to mention a study that was performed before 2010, but the findings were published only in that year.[91] The National Criminology Institute (OKRI) collected data from a Hungarian sample in 2005 as part of two international projects (*International Crime Victimization Survey* and *European Crime and Safety Survey*). The telephone interviews covered issues such as becoming victims of various types of crimes, reporting crime and assumptions about the police. If a respondent decided not to report a crime, the interviewer asked questions about this decision; domestic attitudes toward crime, including fearing crime and the practice of punishing criminals, were explored.

It is again the National Criminology Institute that supported (and again as part of an international, European Council–funded project) a study of the sentiment of insecurity, a key component of the fear of crime. It focused on the social–economic, micro environmental and socio-cultural components of the insecurity that marginal and vulnerable groups felt. Two Budapest districts (Országút and Laposdűlő) produced data, thereby contributing to the international data collected in Barcelona, London, Milan and Paris. We find it exemplary from a methodological perspective that the study combined various types of qualitative (participating observation, in-depth interview and focus group interviews) and quantitative methods were combined. The findings revealed that the insecurity felt by the residents was shaped by economic and environmental factors.[92]

The most important social psychological research in Hungary on legal consciousness in the decade was performed by György Hunyady. This project was particularly relevant for the earlier phases of our project. Hunyady conducted omnibus data collection from a national representative sample first in 2011. The questions covered areas such as social and political attitudes, basic legal principles, the legal system and opinions about compliance with the law. All this was supplemented by a smaller ($n = 240$) survey, involving university graduates, where half of them had a law degree.[93] Two years later, a large number of new items (of a sociopolitical orientation, with special reference to various aspects of the idea of democracy) were added to the questionnaire. For this reason, the analysts could interview two representative samples in 2013. The findings that Hunyady and his group derived from the available, quite extensive data was published in 2015. The volume is a great storehouse of intriguing legal issues, but at this point, we only want to discuss the two chapters that are related to the concept of legal consciousness.

Mihály Berkics's study is closely connected to the 2010 phase of our present project, both thematically and methodologically. It compares the legal conceptions of lawyers and lay people. The study drew on data collection from 2011 and 2013. Conceptions about the law were examined in three thematic categories: basic legal principles (the defense of individual freedom and fundamental rights, the occasionally conflicting elements of the legal system), opinions about courts and the justice system, and questions about the extent to which the respondent and the other members of society ("others") comply with the law. The analysis of the two 2011 samples revealed surprising inconsistencies concerning the opinions about basic legal principles. For example, 73% of the respondents in the representative sample simultaneously agreed with the statements such as "Only people who perform their obligations should have any rights" and "There are human rights that every single person should enjoy equally". The analysts were interested in the reasons for such contradictions, and in an attempt to establish whether the respondents privileged formal justice or substantive justice, the questionnaire for the 2013 representative sample presented various dilemmas to the respondents. According to the conclusion of the project, respondents were likely to prefer liberal legal principles to alternatives promising safety and justice if these principles were exposed in a manner that highlighted their internal contradictions. However, the inconsistencies signaled that these principles did not cohere in the consciousness of the participants unless they were university graduates. At the same time, valuing basic legal principles did not translate into trust in legal institutions and the justice system even on this level. Instead, this kind of trust correlated primarily with political attitudes. When analyzing the answers to the questions about the respondents' own compliance with the law and how they perceive the same issue in the case of "others", the analysts received clearly distorted responses. Many saw themselves as model citizens and suggested that others are quite likely to break the law. Because this erroneous perception did not correlate with any political attitude, the analysts contributed it to the positive self-image of the respondents and their desire to suggest a larger-than-life version of their selves.[94]

Krisztián Pósch's study is also based on the analysis of data from a 2011 representative sample.[95] It focuses on issues such as legal knowledge, support for the core legal principles of democracy and, measuring the perception of procedural justice and relaying on Tyler's theory again, trust in the justice system. The study measured support for the basic values and institutions of democracies with the help of a nine-item scale (where three items reflected negative values), and it measured legal knowledge through the definition of four concepts (the rule of law, positive discrimination, historical constitution and legal certainty). In addition, it measured the perception of procedural justice with the help of a six-statement scale. The analysis demonstrated that there was significant support for the idea of the rule of law, with special regard to general human rights, popular sovereignty and the presumption of innocence. Analyzing the socio-demographic distribution of the answers, it turned out the party preferences show the biggest divergence. Legal knowledge slightly exceeded expectations and, unsurprisingly, it correlated with educational background. However, trust in legal institutions did not correlate with legal knowledge or support for core democratic values. Instead, only party preferences determined it. This finding was just the opposite of a recurring hypothesis in the related literature. Pósch finishes his study with the disturbing conclusion that Hungarian society has very little of the sense of security that could support any kind of trust in the workings of the law.

Tamás Keller's 2014 study should also be mentioned.[96] This project is closely connected, both in terms of its empirical material and its theoretical framework, to István György Tóth's research in 2009.[97] Tóth relied on the data of the fourth and fifth waves of *World Value Survey* and argued that Hungary, with its closed, medium secular-rational character, is far from Western European countries and closer to countries with an orthodox culture such as Bulgaria, the Ukraine or Russia. He also argued that a particular constellation of core values and attitudes will play a crucial role in the possible preservation of this situation. These include the facts that a deficit of trust characterizes Hungarian society; it is less tolerant toward social inequalities; it has an ambivalent relationship with corruption; and it tends to underestimate the tax prices of state services. These value tendencies would not be necessarily pathological in themselves, but in their combination, they generate a self-destructive cycle and threaten the political community, as well as hinder the accumulation of social capital – in other words, these factors decrease institutional and interpersonal trust – and thereby underpin demand for paternalism.

Thus, Keller compared and analyzed the data collected from a 2009 and a 2013 representative sample by reference to the four value categories: trust, corruption, equality and the need for paternalism. During the process, he explored interpersonal trust and institutional trust separately and, in relation to the latter, the perception of institutional corruption. Studying corruption also entails the problem of individual transgression and the support for social norms. The author attempted to measure social backing behind social norms, and he tried to gauge transgressions through the perception of such contrasts as, for example, money made by hard work versus money made by illegal means. In addition, he related assumptions about the value of equality to the need for paternalism. The associated questions concerned differences in wealth and the role that the state played in eliminating these differences. The study also measured opinions about the economic and social activity of the state through comparing these to real market situations. In doing this, the study used housing, agriculture, education, welfare expenses and job creation as separate categories. The compound measures demonstrated a slight positive change in all categories. Keller, however, points out that we need to take these results with reservations. On the one hand, the improvement is not significant; on the other hand, it depends on political orientation to a great extent. All in all, one cannot say that interpersonal and institutional trust actually increased, that corruption is declining, that people are more tolerant toward social differences, or that they privilege market mechanisms over state intervention. What the data really revealed is that a conservative turn has taken place in a thoroughly politicized and polarized society; this turn, however, had only minimal impact on the strength and structure of attitudes.

When discussing trust in the institutions of civil society, we should note two more studies by György Hunyady and Mihály Berkics. Hunyady offers a sophisticated statistical analysis[98] of a rich empirical collection of data in order to explore the influence of the 2010 political crisis and right-wing turn on the structure of the concept of democracy. The study is based on four surveys from the period between 2010 and 2013. Each annual survey is based on a representative sample, where twenty-seven items asked questions about various aspects of democracy, and a 50-statement scale was used to measure opinions about the existing social conditions. When exploring well-known attributes of the concept of democracy, the analysts could identify three major clusters. One group (cluster *z*) is at once characterized by firm belief in high-level democracy and the desire for strong governance. This group shows little resistance to various types of discrimination. The other group (cluster *x*) is characterized by more moderate faith in democracy, but it is also skeptical of centralizing governmental efforts and it clearly rejects social discrimination. It is the third group (cluster *y*) that represents the clearest democratic ideal in that it has high-level support for democracy as a concept and it firmly refuses both centralization and discrimination. The three clusters had more or less equal presence among the respondents, with only "cluster *y*" lagged slightly behind the other two. On a time scale, however, one can see that the number of people belonging to "cluster *x*" nearly doubled and that the number of people belonging to "cluster *y*" dwindled to its half between 2010 and 2013. All in all, Hunyady finds that the link between changes in general thought and attitudes toward the idea of democracy is full of contradictions. As our findings also show, support for the political system coexists with negative, critical attitudes. While it seems that the latter outweighs the former, efforts to support the system aim not at the broader acceptance of democratic ideals but rather at governmental centralization.

Berkics's study[99] focuses on the problem of system justification and, in this connection, he examines issues such as belief in a just world, institutional trust, value structures, fear and the broader acceptance of various legal principles. When exploring system justification, he added a scale to his questionnaire, which made it possible to measure moral outrage and to separate more clearly critical and supportive attitudes toward the political system. The empirical base of the study was the survey modeled upon the two previously mentioned representative samples from 2010 and 2013. As expected, the findings revealed that the dominant attitude in the population is a critical one. The number of the seriously disappointed and very critical grew, even within this short period, from 18.2% (2011) to 23.5% (2013), yet trust in the justice system increased irrespectively of party preferences. Thus, it is clear that the majority of people consider the law to be quite separate from politics. Furthermore, attitudes toward legal principles continue to be quite ambivalent in that they are simultaneously characterized by support for the rule of law and support for harsher punishments for transgressors. This shows the incoherence of the coexisting images about the law, which this book also discusses at length.

Notes

1 An earlier version of the following section has been published as István H. Szilágyi: A jogtudat-kutatások elméleti problématérképe [A Map of the Theoretical Problems of Legal Consciousness Research]. In: H. Szilágyi: *Jogtudat-kutatások Magyarországon 1967–2017* [Legal Consciousness Research in Hungary 1967–2017]. Budapest, Pázmány Press, 2018. 97–122.

2 See Sajó András: Jogi nézetek az egyéni tudatban [Legal Views in the Individual Consciousness]. *Állam- és jogtudomány* (1976) 3. Adam Podgórecki: Public Opinion on Law. In: Adam Podgórecki – Wolfgang Kaupen – Jan van Houtte – Paul Vinke – Berl Kutchinsky: *Knowledge and Opinion about Law*. London, Martin Robertson, 1973. Podgórecki, Adam (1991) *A Sociological Theory of Law*. Milan: Giuffre Editions. Adam Podgórecki: Legal Consciousness as a Research Problem. In: *International Yearbook in Law and Sociology*, 1977. 85–97. In fact, socialist legal sociology existed only in Hungary and Poland because legal sociology could not become part of institutional legal culture in other socialist countries of the era. Cf.: Balázs Fekete – István H. Szilágyi: *Knowledge and Opinion about Law* (KOL) Research in Hungary. 58 *Acta Juridica Hungarica: Hungarian Journal of Legal Studies* (2017) 3, 326–358.

3 For the conceptual development of 'legal pluralism,' see John Griffiths: What Is Legal Pluralism? 28 *Journal of Legal Pluralism* (1989), 1–55. Jacques van der Linden: Return to Legal Pluralism: Twenty Years Later. 28 *Journal of Legal Pluralism* (1989), 148–157.

4 Jean Piaget: The Moral Judgment of the Child. London, Kegan Paul, Trench, Trubner and Co., 1932. Jean Piaget: *Origins of Intelligence in the Child*. London, Routledge & Kegan Paul, 1936.

5 June L. Tapp – Lawrence Kohlberg: Developing Senses of Law and Legal Justice. 27 *Journal of Social Issues* (1971) 2, 65–91. Lawrence Kohlberg: Education, Moral Development and Faith. 4 Journal of Moral Education (1974) 1, 5–16.

6 Albert Bandura: *Social Learning Theory*. Englewood Cliffs, NJ, Prentice Hall, 1977. Ronald L. Akers: *Social Learning and Social Structure: A General Theory of Crime and Deviance*. Boston, Northeastern University Press, 1998.

7 Ellen S. Cohn – Susan O. White: *Legal Socialization: A Study of Norms and Rules*. New York, Springer, 1990.

8 See e.g.: Michele Peterson-Badali: Children's Knowledge of the Legal System: Are They Competent to Instruct Legal Counsel? 34 *Canadian Journal of Criminology* (1992) 2, 139–160. Chantal Kourilsky-Augeven (ed.): *Socialisation juridique et la conscience du droit: Attitudes individuelles, modèles culturels et changement social*. London: Humanities Press, 1983. Paris, LGDJ, Maison des sciences de l'homme, Réseau Européen Droit et Société, 1997. Chantal Kourilsky: Legal Socialization and Cultural Models: Individual Attitudes toward Law in France and Russia. In: *European Yearbook in the Sociology of Law*, 2000. 241–253. Jeffrey Fagan – Tom R. Tyler: Legal Socialization of Children and Adolescents. 18 *Social Justice Research* (2005), 217–241. Rick Trinkner – Tom R. Tyler: Legal Socialization: Coerson versus Consent in an Era of Mistrust. 12 *Annual Review of Law and Social Science* (2016), 417–439. Legal socialization has been cultivated in Hungarian legal sociology since 1970s, both in theoretical and in empirical modes. See: András Sajó: La socialisation juridique en Hongrie sous le communism et après le communisme. 19 *Droit et societé* (1991), 355–363. Ibolya Vári-Szilágyi: Genre et socialisation juridique. Raisonner sur le droit: une différence d'attitude chez les jeunes en Hongrie? 43 *Droit et Cultures* (2002) 1, 59–85. The earlier phases of the current study (Kelemen László – Hollán Miklós, *Joghallgatók a jogról II.* Budapest- Pécs, Dialog Campus, 2013), which explored the legal consciousness of law students, as outlined in the previous chapter, were an integral part of this ongoing research.

9 Stefan Machura – Peter Robson (eds.): *Law and Film*. Oxford, Blackwell Publishers, 2001.

10 Jacquelyn Burkell: Electronic Miscommunication and the Defamatory Sense. 15 *Canadian Journal of Law and Society* (2000) 1, 81–110. Julia Black: Regulatory

Conversations. 29 *Journal of Law and Society* (2002) 1, 163–196. Alan O'Day (ed.): *Cyberterrorism*. Aldershot, Ashgate, 2004. Marc Hertogh: Eric's Day in the Court. In: Marc Hertogh: *Nobody's Law: Legal Consciousness and Legal Alienation in Everyday Life*. London, Palgrave, 2018.

11 Jürgen Habermas: *The Theory of Communicative Action* . Boston, Beacon Press, 1984. Jürgen Habermas: *The Theory of Communicative Action II: System and Lifeworld: A Critique of Functionalist Reason*. Boston, Beacon Press, 1987.

12 Niklas Luhmann: Law as a Social System. 83 *Northwestern University Law Review* (1989) 1–2, 136–150. Niklas Luhmann: Operational Closure and Structural Coupling: The Differentiation of the Legal System. 13 *Cardozo Law Review* (1992), 1419–1441.

13 Günther Teubner: *Law as an Autopoetic System*. Oxford, Blackwell Publishers, 1993.

14 Jacques Derrida: *Writing and Difference*. London, Routledge, 1978.

15 David Nelken: Law as Communication: Constituting the Field. In: David Nelken (ed.): *Law as Communication*. Aldershot, Dartmouth, 1996. 3–23.

16 Peter Goodrich: *Languages of Law: From Logics of Memory to Nomadic Masks*. London, Wiedenfeld & Nicolson, 1990. John Gibbons (ed.): *Language and the Law*. London, Longman, 1994. Lawrence Solan – Peter Tiersma (eds.): *The Oxford Handbook of Language of Law*. Oxford, Oxford University Press, 2012.

17 Bernard Jackson: *Semiotics and Legal Theory*. London, Routlegde & Kegan Paul, 1985. Roberta Kevelson: *The Law as a System of Signs*. New York, Plenum Press, 1988. Bernard Jackson (ed.): *Legal Semiotics and the Sociology of Law*. Oñati, Proceedings of the Oñati Institute, 1994. Anne Wagner – Vijay K. Bhatia (eds.): *Diversity and Tolerance in Socio Legal Context: Explorations in the Semiotics of Law*. Aldershot, Ashegate, 2009.

18 James Boyd White: *The Legal Imagination*. Chicago, University of Chicago Press, 1973. Maria Aristodemou: Studies in Law and Literature: Directions and Concerns. 22 *Anglo-American Law Review* (1993) 2, 157–193. Neil Duxbury: *Law and Letters in American Jurisprudence*. Oxford, Oxford University Press, 1995. Ian Ward: *Law and Literature: Possibilities and Perspective*. Cambridge, Cambridge University Press, 1995. About the Hungraian developments in the field see István H. Szilágyi: Law and Literature in Hungary: An Introduction. 53 *Acta Juridica Hungarica* (2012) 1, 1–6.

19 Eliot E. Slotnick: Media Coverage of Supreme Court Decision-Making: Problems and Prospects. 75 *Judicature* (1991) 3, 128–142. Jan van Dijk: *The Network Society: Social Aspects of New Media*. London, Sage, 1999. Roger Cotterrell: Some Aspects of the Communication of Constitutional Authority. In: Roger Cotterrell: *Living Law: Studies in Legal and Social Theory*. Bulington, Ashgate, 2008. Chapter 15, 257–279. Lieve Gies: *Law and the Media: The Future of an Uneasy Relationship*. New York, Routledge, Cavendish, 2008.

20 Austin Sarat: 'The Law Is All Over': Power Resistance and Legal Consciousness of Welfare Poor. 2 *Yale Journal of Law and Humanities* (1990) 2, 343–379. Alan Reifman: Real Jurors' Understanding of the Law in Real Cases. 16 *Law and Human Behavior* (1992) 5, 539–554. Joachim J. Savelsberg: Knowledge, Domination, and Criminal Punishment. 99 *American Journal of Sociology* (1994) 4, 911–943. Davina Cooper: Local Government: Legal Consciousness in the Shadow of Juridification. 22 *Journal of Law and Society* (1995) 4, 506–526. Robert J. Sampson: Legal Cynicism and (Subcultural?) Tolerance of Deviance: The Neighborhood Context of Racial Differences. 32 *Law & Society Review* (1998) 4, 777–804. Arthur L. Stinchcombe: *When Formality Works: Authority and Abstraction in Law and Organizations*. Chicago, London, The University of Chicago Press, 2001.

21 Richard A. Posner: *The Economics of Justice. Acta Juridica Hungarica, Hungarian Journal of Legal Studies*. Cambridge, MA, London, 1981.

22 Tom R. Tyler: *Why People Obey the Law?* New Haven, London, Yale University Press, 1990.

23 Sally Falk Moore: Law and Social Change: The Semi-Autonomous Social Field as an Appropriate Subject of Study. In: Sally Falk Moore: *Law as Process: An Anthropological Approach*. London, Routledge & Kegan Paul, 1978.

24 Laura NADER: *Harmony Ideology: Justice and Control in a Zapotec Mountain Village*. Stanford, Stanford University Press, 1990.
25 Gabriel A. ALMOND – Sidney VERBA: *The Civic Culture: Political Attitudes and Democracy in Five Nations*. Princeton, Princeton University Press, 1963. 3–43.
26 Austin SARAT – Thomas R. KEARNS (eds.): *Law in Everyday Life*. Ann Arbor, The University of Michigan Press, 1993. William O'BARR – John M. CONLEY: Lay Expectations of the Civil Law Justice System. 22 *Law and Society Review* (1988) 11, 137–171. W. Michael REISMAN: *Law in Brief Encounters*. New Haven, London, Yale University Press, 1999. Patricia EWICK – Susan S. SILBEY: Narrating Social Structure: Stories of Resistance to Legal Authority. 108 *American Journal of Sociology* (2003) 6, 1328–1372. Laura Beth NIELSEN: *License to Harass: Law, Hierarchy, and Offensive Public Speech*. Princeton, Oxford, Princeton University Press, 2004.
27 For an essay toward building up a middle-level theory of non-compliance, see Marc HERTOGH: Loyalists, Legalists, Cynics and Outsiders. In: Marc HERTOGH: *Nobody's Law: Legal Consciousness and Legal Alienation in Everyday Life*. London, Palgrave, 2018. 49–64.
28 See James O. FINCKENAUER: *Russian Youth: Law, Deviance and the Pursuit of Freedom*. New Brunswick, London, Transaction Publishers, 1995. Elijah ANDERSON: *Code of the Street: Decency, Violence, and the Moral Life of the Inner City*. Norton: W. W. Norton & Company, 2000. Ronald L. AKERS – Gary F. JENSEN: *The Empirical Status of Social Learning Theory of Crime and Deviance: The Past, Present, and Future*. In: Francis T. CULLEN – John Paul WRIGHT – Kristie R. BLEVINS (eds.): *Advances in Criminological Theory. Vol. 15: Taking Stock: The Status of Criminological Theory*. New Brunswick, Transaction Publishers, 2006. 37–76. Richard McMAHON (ed.): *Crime, Law and Popular Culture in Europe, 1500–1900*. Devon, Portland, Willan Publishing, 2008.
29 Robert H. MNOOKIN – Lewis KORNHAUSER: Bargaining in the Shadow of the Law: The Case of Divorce. 88 *Yale Law Journal* (1979) 5, 950–997.
30 Henry S. FARBER – Michelle J. WHITE: A Comparison of Formal and Informal Dispute Resolution in Medical Malpractice. 23 *Journal of Legal Studies* (1994) 2, 777–806. Calvin MORRILL: Institutional Change through Interstitial Emergence: The Growth of Alternative Dispute Resolution in American Law, 1965–1995. 4 *Revista de Estudos Empíricos em Direito* (2017) 1, 1–44.
31 Kimmett EDGAR – Tim NEWELL: *Restorative Justice in Prisons: A Guide to Making It Happen*. Winchester, Waterside Press, 2006. Holly Ventura MILLER (ed.): *Restorative Justice: From Theory to Practice: Sociology of Crime, Law, and Deviance*. Vol. 5. Bingley, Emerald Publishing Ltd., 2008.
32 Eugen EHRLICH: *Fundamental Principles of the Sociology of Law*. Cambridge, MA, Harvard University Press, 1936.
33 John GRIFFITHS: The Social Working of Legal Rules. 35 *Journal of Legal Pluralism* (2003) 48, 1–84.
34 András SAJÓ: *A jogosultság-tudat vizsgálata. Kutatási összefoglaló* [The Study of Rights Consciousness: Research Summary]. Budapest, MTA Állam- és Jogtudományi Intézete [manuscript], 1988. Patricia EWICK – Susan S. SYLBEY: *The Common Place of Law: Stories from Everyday Life*. Chicago, Chicago University Press, 1998.
35 Ibid.
36 Irene STYLES: Law Clinics and the Promotion of Public Interest Lawyering. 19 *Law in Context* (2001) 1–2, 65–88. Frank MUNGER (ed.): *Law and Poverty*. Aldershot, Ashgate, 2006. Diana HERNÁNDEZ: 'I'm Gonna Call My Laywer': Shifting Legal Consciousness at the Intersection of Inequality. 51 *Studies in Law, Politics, and Society* (2010), 95–121.
37 Setsuo MIYAZAWA: Taking Kawashima Seriously: A Review of Japanese Research on Japanese Legal Consciousness and Disputing Behavior. 21 *Law and Society Review* (1987) 2, 219–241. Erhadt BLANKENBURG: The Infrastucture for Avoiding Civil Litigation: Comparing Cultures of Legal Behaviour in the Netherlands and Germany. 28 *Law*

& Society Review (1994) 4, 789–809. Erhardt BLANKENBURG: Civil Litigation Rates as Indicators for Legal Cultures. In: David NELKEN (ed.): *Comparing Legal Cultures*. Aldershot, Dartmouth, 1997. 41–68. Masayuki MURAYAMA: Kawashima and the Changing Focus on Japanese Legal Consciousness: A Selective History of the Sociology of Law in Japan. 9 *International Journal of Law in Context* (2013) 4, 565–589. Marc HERTOGH: The Myth of Dutch Legal Culture. In: Marc HERTOGH: *Nobody's Law: Legal Consciousness and Legal Alienation in Everyday Life*. London, Palgrave, 2018. 27–48.

38 Lawrence M. FRIEDMAN: *The Legal System: A Social Science Perspective*. New York, Russel Sage Foundation, 1975. 1–24.

39 BLANKENBURG: The Infrastucture for Avoiding Civil Litigation.

40 Martin KRYGIER: The Infrastucture for Avoiding Civil Litigation. Martin KRYGIER: The Rule of Law: Legality, Teleology, Sociology. In: Gianluigi PALOMBELLA – Neil WALKER (eds.): *Relocating the Rule of Law. Acta Juridica Hungarica, Hungarian Journal of Legal Studies*. Oxford, Hart Publishing, 2009. 45–69.

41 FRIEDMAN: *The Legal System*. 15–16, 193–222, 223–268. For a concise summary of the scholarly debate that has unfolded about the concept of legal culture see: David NELKEN: Disclosing/Invoking Legal Culture: An Introduction. 4 *Social & Legal Studies* (1995), 435–452. Susan S. SILBEY: Legal Culture and Legal Consciousness. In: *International Encyclopedia of the Social and Behavioral Sciences*. Elsevier, The University of Chicago Press, 2001. 8623–8629, 8624–8626. Marina KURKCHIYAN: Russian Legal Culture: An Analysis of Adaptive Response to an Institutional Transplant. 34 *Law & Social Inquiry* (2009) 2, 337–364, 337–338.

42 Roger COTTERRELL: *Law, Culture & Society*. Burlington, Ashgate, 2006. 81–108, 83–88.

43 GRIFFITHS: The Social Working of Legal Rules.

44 PODGÓRECKI et al.: *Knowledge and Opinion about Law*.

45 György GAJDUSCHEK – Balázs FEKETE: Changes in the Knowledge about the Law in Hungary in the Past Half Century. 57 *Sociologija* (2015) 4. Paper 636.

46 We use the phrase "world view" in its broadest possible sense, including, for example, political orientation and even ideologies associated with various fan clubs.

47 Richard D. SCHWARTZ: Social Factors in the Development of Social Control: A Case Study of Two Israeli Settlements. 63 *Yale Law Journal* (1954) 4, 471–491.

48 Jane F. COLLIER: Stratification and Dispute Handling in Two Highland Chiapas Communities. 6 *American Ethnologist* (1979) 2, 305–327.

49 SCHWARTZ: Social Factors in the Development of Social Control. 471–491. COLLIER: Stratification and Dispute Handling in Two Highland Chiapas Communities. 305–327. Mark KESSLER: The Politics of Legal Representation: The Influence of Local Politics on the Behavior of Poverty Lawyers. 8 *Law & Policy* (1986) 2, 149–168. Carol J. GREENHOUSE – Barbara YNGVESSON – David M. ENGEL: *Law and Community in Three American Towns*. Ithaca, London, Cornell University Press, 1994. Hungarian studies in this field do not really exist. They could not be conducted for political-ideological reasons before the late 1980s. Afterwards, no one embarked on such projects with the important exception of the pioneering scholarship of Sándor Loss. Sándor Loss: *Romani kris* a dél-békési oláhcigányoknál. Elmélet és gyakorlat [*Romani Kris* among the Vlach Gypsies of South Békés County: Theory and Practice]. In: Miklós SZABÓ (ed.): *Ius Humanum: Az ember alkotta jog* [The Man Made Law]. Miskolc, Bíbor Kiadó, 2001. 9–22.

50 Jan van HOUTTE – Paul VINKE: Attitudes Governing the Acceptance of Legislation among Various Social Groups. In: PODGÓRECKI et al.: *Knowledge and Opinion about Law*.

51 John MORISON – Philip LEITH – Milton KEYNES: *The Barrister's World and the Nature of Law*. Philadelphia, Open University Press, 1991. Robert A. KATZMANN: *The Law Firm and the Public Good*. Washington, DC, The Brookings Institution, 1995. Richard L. ABEL (ed.): *Lawyers: A Critical Reader*. New York, The New Press, 1997. W. Wesley PUE – David SUGARMAN (ed.): *Lawyers and Vampires: Cultural Histories of Legal Professions*. Oxford, Portland, Hart Publishing, 2003.

52 Ágnes UTASI (ed.): *Az ügyvédek hivatásrendje* [The Professional Order of Attorneys]. Budapest, Új Mandátum, 1999. Ágnes UTASI (ed.): *Ügyvédek a gyorsuló időben (1998–2015)* [Attorneys in Quickening Time]. Szeged, Belvedere Meridionale, 2016. István H. SZILÁGYI – Andrea JANKÓ-BADÓ: Further Thoughts on the Self-Image of the Hungarian Attorneys. 1 *International Journal of Law and Society* (2018) 4, 137–149.
53 Cf.: FRIEDMAN: *The Legal System*. 223. See also Lawrence M. FRIEDMAN: *Law and Society: An Introduction*. Englewood Cliffs, NY, Prentice Hall, 1977. 76. Lawrence M. FRIEDMAN: *The Republic of Choice: Law, Authority, and Culture*. Cambridge, MA, Harvard University Press, 1990. 4.
54 SZILÁGYI – JANKÓ-BADÓ: Further Thoughts on the Self-Image of the Hungarian Attorneys.
55 Cf. Robert M. COVER: The Supreme Court, 1982 Term: Foreword: Nomos and Narrative. 97 *Harvard Law Review* 4 (1983).
56 This is how the honest attorney, Petrocelli, the protagonist of an American TV show who defends the rights of his clients to the very end will be the pun for a sarcastic moniker for the Hungarian attorney representing Roma rights, Putricelli (the first part of the name, "putri" stands for the gypsy hut). Cf. István H. SZILÁGYI: There Is No Mercy. 56 *Acta Juridica Hungarica* (2015) 1, 86–107.
57 Balazs FEKETE – Gyorgy GAJDUSCHEK: Changes in Knowledge about Law in Hungary in the Past Half Century. 57 *Sociologija* (2015) 4, 620–636. Available at SSRN: https://ssrn.com/abstract=2794812
58 Mihály BERKICS: Laikusok és jogászok nézetei a jogról; Rendszer és jogrendszer percepciói Magyarországon [Laymen's and Lawyers' Views on Law: Perception of Order and Legal System in Hungary]. In: György HUNYADY – Mihály BERKICS (eds.): *A jog szociálpszichológiája. A hiányzó láncszem* [Social Psychology of Law: The Missing Link]. Budapest, ELTE Eötvös Kiadó, 2015. 141–160, 337–364.
59 Berl KUTCHINSKY: The Legal Consciousness. In: PODGÓRECKI et al.: *Knowledge and Opinion about Law*.
60 Vilhelm AUBERT: Resarches in the Sociology of Law. 7 *American Behavioral Scientist* (1963) 4, 16–20. Donald J. BLACK: The Mobilization of Law. 2 *Journal of Legal Studies* (1973) 1, 125–149. Mariana VALVERDE: *Law's Dream of a Common Knowledge*. Princeton, Oxford, Princeton University Press, 2003.
61 Hungarian legal consciousness research has confirmed these findings repeatedly. FEKETE – GAJDUSCHEK: Changes in Knowledge About Law in Hungary in the Past Half Century.
62 TYLER: *Why People Obey the Law?*
63 Cf.: Rüdiger SCHOTT: Main Trends in German Ethnological Jurisprudence. 20 *Journal of Legal Pluralism* (1982) 14, 37–68.
64 Arnold GEHLEN: *Man: His Nature and Place in the World* [1943] (Trans: C. MCMILLAN – K. PILLEMER). New York, Columbia University Press, 1987. Peter L. BERGER – Hansfried KELLNER: Arnold Gehlen and the Theory of Institutions. 32 *Social Research* (1965) 1, 110–115.
65 Konrad LORENZ: *The Civilized Man' Eight Deadly Sins*. New York, Harcourt Brace Jovanovich, Inc., 1974.
66 András SAJÓ: *Constitutional Sentiments*. New Haven, Yale University, 2010.
67 András SAJÓ – Mária SZÉKELYI – Péter MAJOR: *Vizsgálat a fizikai dolgozók jogtudatáról* [Study in the Legal Consciousness of Manual Workers]. Budapest, MTA ÁJTI, 1977.
68 Jon ELSTER: Myopia and Foresight. In: Jon ELSTER: *Explaining Social Behaviour: More Nuts and Bolts for the Social Sciences*. Cambridge, Cambridge University Press, 2015. 99–113.
69 Gordon W. ALLPORT: Attitudes. In: Carl MURCHISON (ed.): *A Handbook of Social Psychology*. Worcester, MA, Clark University Press, 1935. 789–844.
70 Neil VILDMAR: Generic Prejudice and the Presumption of Guilt in Sex Abuse Trials. 21 *Law and Human Behavior* (1997) 1, 5–25. Dennis R. FOX: Psycholegal Scholarship's Contribution to False Consciousness about Injustice. 23 *Law and Human Behavior*

(1999) 1, 9–30. Reisman: *Law in Brief Encounters*. Virginia Sapiro: Gender Equality in the Public Mind. 22 *Women & Politics* (2001) 1, 1–36.

Michelle D. St. Amand: Impact of Information about Sentencing Decisions on Public Attitudes toward the Criminal Justice System. 25 *Law and Human Behavior* (2001) 5, 515–528.

71 Berkics: Laikusok és jogászok nézetei a jogról. 141–160, 337–364.

72 See Jan-Erik Lönnquist – Zsolt Péter Szabó – Laszlo Kelemen: Rigidity of the Far-Right? Motivated Social Cognition in a Nationally Representative Sample of Hungarians on the Eve of the Far-Right Breakthrough in the 2010 Elections. 54 *International Journal of Psychology* (2019) 3, 292–296.

73 Rokumoto, Kahei 六本佳平: *Nihon no hō to shakai* 日本の法と社会 [The Japanese Law and Society]. Tokyo, Yūhikaku 有斐閣, 2004.

74 Cf.: Masayuki Murayama: Culture, Situation and Behaviour. In: Dimitri Vanorverbeke – Jaroen Maesschalck – David Nelken – Stephan Parmentier: *The Changing Role of Law in Japan*. Cheltenem, UK, Northampton, MA, USA, Edward Elgar Publishing, 2014. 189–205, 191.

75 Marc Hertogh: A 'European' Concept of Legal Consciousness: Rediscovering Eugen Ehrlich. 31 *Journal of Law & Society Review* (2004) 4, 457–481.

76 Ld.: Roscoe Pound: Law in Books and Law in Action. 44 *American Law Review* (1910) 12.

77 Ld.: Eugen Ehrlich: The Sociology of Law. 36 *Harvard Law Review* (1920), 130. Eugen Ehrlich: Das lebende Recht der Völker der Bukowina. 1 *Recht und Wirtshaft* (1912).

78 Marc Hertogh: *Nobody's Law: Legal Consciousness and Legal Alienation in Everyday Life*. London, Palgrave, 2018. 1–15.

79 Ld. pl.: Marc Galanter: Why the 'Haves' Come Out Ahead: Speculations on the Limits of Legal Change. 9 *Lawc Society Review* (1974) 1, 95–160. Marc Galanter: Justice in Many Rooms: Courts, Private Ordering, and Indigenous Law, 2013. 13 *Journal of Legal Pluralism and Unioff icial Law* 19, 1–47. Sally Engle Merry: *Getting Justice and Getting Even: Legal Consciousness among Working-Class American*. Chicago, Chicago University Press, 1990. Ewick – Sylbey: *The Common Place of Law*. David Engel: How Does Law Matter? In the Constitution of Legal Consciousness? In: B. Garth – Austin Sarat: *How Does Law Matter?* Chicago, Northwestern University Press, 1998. 109–144. Laura Beth Nielsen: Situating Legal Consciousness: Experiences and Attitudes of Ordinary Citizens about Law and Street Harassment. 34 *Law & Society Review* (2000) 4, 1055–1090.

80 It is hard to mistake the irony in the term "secular", given the Marxist affiliation of representatives of the "critical" approach.

81 Róbert Richard Kiss – Ágnes Zsidai: *Társadalom és jog* [Society and Law]. Budapest, GloboBook Kiadó, 2016.

82 See Zoltán Fleck – Valéria Kiss – Fruzsina Tóth – László Neumann – Anikó Kenéz – Dávid Bajnok: *A jogtudat narratív elemzése* [A Narrative Analyisy of the Legal Consciousness]. Budapest, ELTE Eötvös Kiadó, 2017.

83 Gajduschek – Fekete: Changes in the Knowledge about the Law in Hungary in the Past Half Century.

84 István H. Szilágyi István – György Gajduschek: Nevelés és büntetés [Child Rearing and Punishment]. In: H. Szilágyi: *Jogtudat-kutatások Magyarországon*. 221–238.

85 James L. Gibson – Gregory A. Caldeira: The Legal Cultures of Europe. 30 *Law & Society Review* (1996) 1, 55–85.

86 Balazs Fekete – Peter Robert: Understanding Hungarian Attitudes toward Law in an International Context (February 9, 2018). SSRN: https://ssrn.com/abstract=3120933 or http://dx.doi.org/10.2139/ssrn.3120933

87 Zsolt Boda: Bizalom, legitimitás és jogkövetés. In: H. Szilágyi: *Jogtudat-kutatások Magyarországon*. 255–278.

88 György Gajduschek: Miért engedelmeskednek az emberek a dohányzást tiltó jognak? [Why Do People Obey the Law Prohibiting Smoking?]. In: H. Szilágyi: *Jogtudat-kutatások Magyarországon 1967–2017*. 279–302.
89 Péter Róbert – Balázs Fekete: Ki ellen nyerne meg ön egy pert? [Against Whom Would You Win a Case?]. In: H. Szilágyi: *Jogtudat-kutatások Magyarországon 1967–2017*. 303–322.
90 András Jakab – György Gajduschek: The Rule of Law, Legal Consciousness and Compliance. In: *Hungarian Social Report 2019*. Budapest, TÁRKI, 2019. 277–294.
91 Klára Kerezsi – József Kó: Az áldozattá válás jellemzői Magyarországon a 2005-ös viktimológiai felmérés tükrében [Characteristics of Victimization in the Mirror of the 2005 Survey on Victimology]. In: György Virág (ed.): *Kriminológiai Tanulmányok 47* [Crimological Studies]. Budapest, OKRI, 2010. 113–130.
92 Andrea Tünde Barabás (ed.): *The Dimensions of Insecurity in Urban Areas: Research on the Roots of Unsafety and Fear of Crime in European Cities*. Budapest, OKRI, 2018.
93 Mihály Berkics – György Hunyady (eds.): *A jog és pszichológia: egy interdiszciplináris mező* [Law and Psychology: An Interdisciplinary Field]. Budapest, ELTE Eötvös Kiadó, 2012.
94 Berkics: Laikusok és jogászok nézetei a jogról.
95 Krisztián Pósch: Jogismeret, a demokratikus értékek támogatottsága és a procedurális igazságossággal kapcsolatos nézetek a mai magyar társadalomban [Knowledge of Law, Support of Democratic Values and Views about Procedural Justice in Contemporary Hungary]. In: Hunyady – Berkics: *A jog szociálpszichológiája*. 161–176.
96 Tamás Keller: Megfogyva bár, de törve . . . Mérsékelten javuló mutatók, súlyosan növekvő politikai polarizáltság a magyar értékrendszerben, változások 2009 és 20013 között [Lost But Not Crushed . . . Moderately Improving Indexes, Heavily Increasing Political Polarization in the Hungarian Value System: Changes between 2009 and 2012]. In: Tamás Kolosi – István György Tóth (eds.): *Társadalmi Riport 2014* [Social Report 2014]. Budapest, TÁRKI, 2014. 375–403.
97 István György Tóth: *Bizalomhiány, normazavarok, igazságtalanságérzet és paternalizmus a magyar társadalom értékszerkezetében. A gazdasági felemelkedés, társadalmi-kulturális feltételei című kutatás zárójelentése* [Summary Report of the 'Social and Cultural Conditions of Economic Improvement' Research Project (Social and Cultural Anomalies)]. Budapest, TÁRKI, 2009. http://mek.oszk.hu/13400/13432/13432.pdf
98 György Hunyady: Demokrácia-követelmények a köztudatban és a társadalmi atmoszféra ambivalenciája [Democratic Requirements in the Public Opinion and the Ambivalence of the Social Atmosphere]. In: Hunyady – Berkics: *A jog szociálpszichológiája*. 281–335.
99 Berkics: Rendszer és jogrendszer percepciói Magyarországon.

3 Methodology

The methodological background of this book is a descriptive-explorative one. Questionnaires were used to identify and understand a number of social phenomena. A large amount of data emerged from the sample that consisted of a total of 1,000 respondents, which demanded thorough statistical processing.

3.1 The questionnaire

Data collection was based on the questionnaire in Appendix No. 2. Apart from very minor modifications, this questionnaire is identical with the one used during the 2010 data collection, which made it possible to compare and contrast the data from the two time periods and isolate the changes that took place. The structure of the questionnaire and the legal scholarship behind it was the following:

Questions No. 1–6 registered the demographical characteristics of the respondents, such as age, gender, place of residence and educational background.
Question No. 7 was about the respondents' receptivity to political issues. Our earlier research indicated that this question can contribute to the creation of a measure.[1]
Questions No. 8.1, 9.1 and 10.1 were designed to map the respondents' sources of information. It was also here that through offering the respondents a selection of print and online media platforms, these persons' objective political orientation was identified.
Questions No. 8.2, 8.3, 9.2, 9.3, 10.2 and 10.3 probed into the assumed credibility of a given medium, enabling the analysts to create a so-called "information-credibility measure".

Scale No. 11 on the questionnaire was designed to measure the extent to which the respondents are critical of the political regime (System Criticism scale).[2] This scale can be brought into an analogy with scale No. 18, which is about the opposite attitude, support for the regime. On the regime criticism scale, statements No. 11.2, 11.4, 11.6 and 11.7 receive inverted scores. Statements on scale No. 12.1 raise issues that have always attracted a great deal of publicity, such as the reestablishment of the death penalty, the prohibition of abortion, the legalization of milder drugs and a harsher sentencing; these items appeared also in earlier questionnaires, so we were able to contrast them with the new findings.

Question No. 12.2 was interested in the motivation behind attitudes supporting or rejecting the death penalty. This question was borrowed from a 2015 questionnaire, which was also conducted from a representative sample.

Scale No. 13 was also used earlier when it measured the respondents' satisfaction with the justice system.

Scale No. 14 concerned itself with causes of criminality. During the process, law students answered open questions, then the contents were analyzed. Then the participants were requested to rank these causes. As in the 2010 study, the measured results were placed in a four-tier Likert scale. At the same time, the participants were requested to list the three most important causes behind criminal behavior.

Questions No. 15.1 and 15.2 probed into sentiments about the current crime rate. These too appeared in earlier questionnaires.

Scale No. 16 was about various opinions about crime prevention. It was created in the first phase of the project along with getting basic information about the law students.

Scale No. 17 is the so-called Just World Beliefs Scale. Its creation was inspired, among others, by the research of Claudia Dalbert and Berkics.[3] Statements No. 1, 2, 5 and 6 on the scale contained "general" observations, while statements No. 3, 4, 7 and 8 carried "person-specific" observations.

When editing scale No. 18 – which is the counterpart to the "regime criticism" scale No. 11 – our starting point was the eight-statement System Justification Scale of Jost and Kay. In addition, we included insights from József Forgács and Berkics.[4] Statements No. 2 and 6 have inverted scoring.

Scale No. 19 explored the valuation of the principles of equity and equality. This is the so-called Equity/Equality Values Scale. Its eight-statement, four-tier Likert scale was specified by Forgács, while the Hungarian version of the applied set of items was derived from the lectures of Berkics and Balázs Bíró.[5] Statements No. 1 and 2 are the "equity" items, whereas the "equality" ones are statements No. 3 and 4. Items No. 2 and 4 carry inverted scoring.

Scales No. 20.1 and 20.2 measure the phenomenon of alienation. The first (20.1) is based on Dwight G. Dean's original Alienation Scale.[6] This includes the three components of powerlessness, normlessness and social isolation. Item No. 1 is about powerlessness, No. 2 and 3 are about normlessness and No. 4 and 5 are about isolation. Statement No. 4 has inverted scoring. The second (20.2) scale is based on Leo Srole's classical, five-item set of questions.[7]

Scales No. 21, 22 and 23 are based on the contributions of Marilynn Brewer.[8] Scale No. 21 is the Globalization and Human Cooperation scale and it raises questions about how humans can cooperate in an increasingly globalized world. Items 21.3 and 21.4

are not parts of the original listing. Scale No. 22 examines the respondents' relatedness to various groups and communities. It is based partly on Forgács's work, partly on our own ideas. Scale No. 23 explores the respondent's sentiments about globalization. This too relies on Forgács's ideas. During the process, we highlighted statement No. 5 where respondents face the claim that globalization has a negative influence on crime. Items 1, 3 and 5 had inverted scoring because they contrasted "cosmopolitanism" with "particularism" and "localism". The items on scale No. 24 have been selected from Morris Rosenberg's ten-statement, four-tier Self-Esteem Scale.[9] Statements 2, 3 and 5 have inverted scoring, while item 4 checks how truthfully a given respondent replied. Thinking style was measured by scale No. 25. In creating this scale, we narrowed down the eighteen statements of John T. Cacioppo's Need for Cognition Scale[10] to five items. Scale No. 26 showed interest in how closed or how open was a given respondents' thinking style. Following Forgács's guidance, we used six statements from the original forty-seven on the original Webster-Kruglanski Need for Closure Scale.[11] Statements 2 and 5 have inverted scoring, whereas items 3 and 6 check how truthfully a given respondent replied.

Scale No. 27 aimed to map the authoritarian personality traits in the respondents. This kind of research began after World War II with the pioneering contribution of Theodor Adorno and his colleagues.[12] Adorno's classic F-Scale became the basis for Anesi's thirty-statement, six-tier scale.[13]

Scale No. 28 is a Hungarian-language version of the so-called Ten-Item Personality Inventory (TIPI),[14] where statements 1 and 6 correspond to Extraversion, 2 and 7 to Agreeableness, 3 and 8 to Conscientiousness, 4 and 9 to Emotional Stability and 5 and 7 to Openness to Experiences. Items 2, 4, 6 and 8 have inverted scoring. Another possibility to map personality traits would have been to use Goldberg's fifty-item, five-tier scale[15]; however, the length of the questionnaire rendered TIPI a more appropriate choice.

Scale No. 29 had again a demographic character in that it collected data about the respondents' family background. Item 30 was designed to find out about the employee status of respondents and their spouses, item 31 measured the respondents' net income per capita and item 32 was interested in the subjective evaluation of one's financial background. Scale No. 33 measured the time that the respondents spend online, supplementing thereby the scope of the also internet-related item 10. Scale No. 34 asked whether the respondent ever became the victim of crime. This item is connected to question No. 12.5 on the questionnaire through the assumption that becoming a victim creates a stronger demand for harsher punishment.

3.2 The sample

Our research relied on a 1,000-person national representative sample. The necessary fieldwork for the survey was performed in November and December of 2018. A well-established market research company with a specialization in fieldwork helped with the process. The representativeness of the sample was achieved by quota tables with four categories (gender, age, type of settlement and county). The Standard Random Progression method was also deployed. The entire procedure was conducted in accordance with the rules of professional market research. After collecting and double-checking the data, the pollsters transferred data into the appropriate templates, creating a database in Excel format and labeled SPSS files.

3.3 Key aspects of data processing

The program IBM SPSS Statistics version 25 was used for processing the data that had been collected. The questionnaires themselves were designed in a way that aimed at the unambiguous equation between questions and statistical variables. Each question appeared with an individual serial number, and the questionnaire contained codes that corresponded to answers. Adding the letter "*k*" to the serial number of the questions, the names of the variables could be derived, and the labels of the variables could be derived from their texts. Thus, both the values of the variables and the labels designating the contents of the variables corresponded to specific questions, without any ambiguity.

Checking the data, labeling and cleaning them were completed with the labeling and transformational commands of the SPSS program. New variables emerged from the variables corresponding to core data. Naming and labeling these were done in a way that again contained reference to the origin of these variables. First, statistical tables were created containing original and calculated variables. Correlation and differences between groups were examined through the following mathematical statistical procedures: c2, correlation, Z-probe and T-probe. When analyzing the findings, these aspects of variable creation proved particularly useful.

During the analysis of differences in percentage, mid-values and correlational coefficiencies, the following considerations are relevant:

1 Working with 1,000 items, 3.1% difference and 0.01 correlation produces 5% mathematical significance.
2 The significance level had to be modified for numerous comparisons because in the case of 100 comparisons, approximately 5% could produce erroneously significant results. Mathematicians have various methods to eliminate such errors, the best-known procedure (Bonferroni) is to divide the significance level value by the number of comparisons.
3 Mathematical significance and empirically significant difference or correlation are not the same concepts. In other words, one should attribute significance to a given difference or correlation only if it is noteworthy, academically and empirically.

Notes

1 Kelemen László – Hollán Miklós, *Joghallgatók a jogról II.* Budapest- Pécs, Dialog Campus, 2013
2 This scale is based on the publications of József Forgács (2009) and a conference presentation of Mihály Berkics (2006). Berkics Mihály: Az igazságtalan világba vetett hit, avagy a cinizmus, a társadalmi kohézió és a társadalom-politikai részvétel szociálpszichológiájáról (lecture). *MPT Országos Tudományos Nagygyűlése*, Budapest, 2006.

3 Claudia DALBERT: Beliefs in a Just World Questionnaire. In: John MALTBY – Christopher Alan LEWIS – Andrew HILL (eds.): *Comissioned Reviews of 250 Psychological Tests*. Lewiston, NY, Mellen Press, 2000. 461–465. BERKICS: Az igazságtalan világba vetett hit. A. Y. MOUS: *Belief in a Just World: How Our Perceptions Impact Our Judgements*. Valdosta, Valdosta University, 2000.

4 Especially John T. JOST – Alison LEDGERWOOD – Curtis D. HARDIN: Shared Reality, System Justification, and Realational Bases of Ideological Beliefs. 1 *Social and Personality Psychological Compass* (2007) 1, 1–16. John T. JOST – Orsolya HUNYADY: The Psychology of System Justification and the Palliative Function of Ideology. 13 *European Review of Social Psychology* (2002) 1, 113–153. Micahel DAMBRUN: Gender Differences in Mental Health: The Mediating Role of Percived Personal Discrimination. 37 *Journal of Applied Social Psychology* (2007) 5, 1118–1129. Aaron C. KAY – John T. JOST – Sean YOUNG: Victim Derogation and Victim Enhancement as Alternate Routes to System Justification. 16 *Psychological Science* (2005) 3, 240–246. Brenda MAJOR – Sarah S. M. TOWNSEND: Psychological Implications of Attitudes and Beliefs about Status Inequality. In: Joseph FORGAS – Joel COOPER – William D CRANO (eds.): *The Psychology of Attitudes and Attitude Change*. New York, London, Psychology Press, 2010. 249–262.

5 Mihály BERKICS – Balázs BÍRÓ: Rendszerigazolás vagy rendszerkritika. A rendszerigazolási elmélet magyarországi alkalmazhatóságának vizsgálata a méltányosságra és az igazságosságra vonatkozó percepciók tükrében (lecture). *MPT XVII. Országos Tudományos Nagygyűlése*, Budapest, 2006.

6 Dwight G. DEAN: Alienation: Its Meaning and Measurement. 26 *American Sociological Review* (1961) 5, 753–758.

7 Leo SROLE: Social Integration and Certain Corollaries: An Exploratory Study. 21 *American Sociological Review* (1956), 709–716.

8 Marilynn BREWER: Depersonalised Trust and Ingroup Cooperation. In: J. KRUEGER (ed.): *Rationality and Social Responsibility*. New York, London, Psychology Press, 2008. 215–232. Nancy R. BUCHAN – Gianluca GRIMALDO – Rick WILSON – Marilynn BREWER – Enrique FATAS – Margaret FODDY: Globalization and Human Cooperation. 106 *PNAS* (2009) 11, 4138–4142.

9 See Morris ROSENBERG: *Society and the Adolescent Self-Image*. Princeton, NJ, Princeton University Press, 1965.

10 John T. CACIOPPO – Richard E. PETTY: The Need for Cognition. 42 *Journal of Personality and Social Psychology* (1982) 1, 116–131.

11 Donna M. WEBSTER – Arie W. KRUGLANSKI: Individual Differences in Need for Cognitive Closure. 67 *Journal of Personality and Social Psychology* (1994) 6, 1049–1062.

12 Theodor W. ADORNO – Else FRENKEL-BRUNSWIK – Daniel LEWINSON – Newitt SANFORD: *The Authoritarian Personality*. New York, Harper & Brothers, 1950.

13 Chuck ANESI: *The F Scale* (1997). www.anesi.com/fscale.htm

14 Samuel D. GOSLING – Jason RENTFROW – William B. SWANN: A Very Brief Measure of the Big-Five Personality Domains. 37 *Journal of Research in Personality* (2003) 6, 504–528.

15 Lewis R. GOLDBERG: The Development of Markers for the Big-Five Factor Structure. 4 *Psychological Assessment* (1992) 1, 26–42.

4 Survey findings

4.1 Socio-demographic characteristics of the sample

47% of women and 53% of men make up the total number of respondents. 4 % represents the youngest age group (18- to 19-year-olds) in the sample. Breaking down the 20- to 59-year-olds into 10-year age groups, we see that their ratio is roughly identical, not reaching 20%. The 20- to 29-year-olds and 30- to 39-year-olds make up 19%, 40- to 49-year-olds represent 17%, whereas 50- to 59-year-olds constitute 18% of the sample. The two oldest age groups have a lower ratio: 13% include 60- to 69-year-olds and 10% include 70- to 79-year-olds. 18% of the respondents live in Budapest, a further 20% in regional capitals.[1] 30% reside in other towns. Nearly one-third of the respondents live in villages.

We surveyed the financial situation of the respondents through two questions. The first question was about monthly net income per capita in one household. Similarly to other empirical studies, a large number of respondents refused to provide this data. Because of this difficulty, we used a variable to measure subjectively perceived financial situation (Figure 4.1).

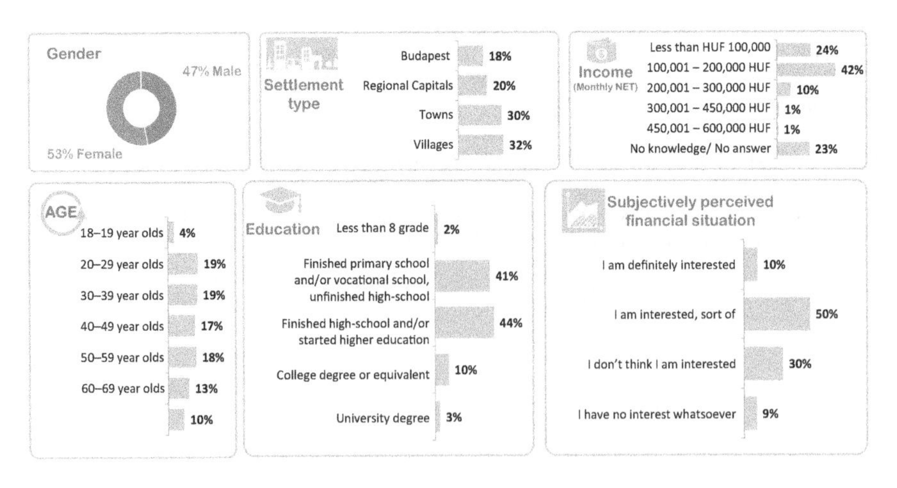

Figure 4.1 Socio-demographic characteristics of the sample

About one-quarter of the participants refused to respond to questions about their financial situation. A similar rate (24%) claimed that their monthly net income per capita does not reach 100,000 HUF ($336). 42% indicated that for them this amount is between 100,000 HUF and 200,000 HUF ($336-$672). One in ten people identified this amount as between 200,000 and 300,000 HUF ($672-$1,009). Only 2% reported having a higher income.

5% of the respondents responded: "I can afford essentially everything" on the scale about subjectively perceived financial situation. Two-thirds of the participants chose, "I do relatively well, but I am aware of my limits". One-quarter of the sample is in a more difficult situation, so they chose: "There are things I can't afford, I run out of money by the end of the month". 3% reported being in a very difficult financial situation.

4.2 Interest in topical social issues

To varying degrees, 60% of the respondents express their interest in topical social issues; 10% reported a strong interest; and 30% expressed hardly any interest. Nearly 10% claimed almost total detachment from these issues.

4.3 Sources of information and their credibility

When exploring general interest in social issues, it is clearly relevant to ask respondents what sources of information they rely on. Because the Hungarian media market has undergone significant changes since 2010 and a given media outlet could represent quite different political orientations during this period, it is difficult to compare the data (e.g. the size of readership or their reliability) accurately, especially given how much more prevalent social media has become. To survey key

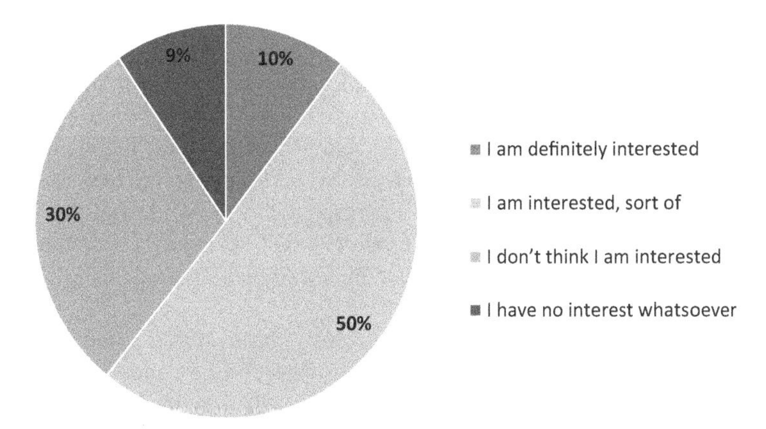

Figure 4.2 Interest in topical social issues

sources of information, we studied dailies and weeklies, television news programs and websites, including Facebook. Respondents were asked to assess the reliability of these sources. In addition, they were requested to provide the average amount of time they spend online on weekdays and weekends and indicate whether they use the internet on these occasions for work or other purposes (Figure 4.2).

The press

In the category of printed newspapers, sensational papers and the free *Lokál* (right-wing tabloid) attract the highest number of readers. 21% of the respondents read *Blikk* (right-wing tabloid), followed by *Story* (independent tabloid) (13%), *Bors* (right-wing tabloid) (11%) and *Lokál* (6%). *HVG* (liberal news magazine) is the most popular specifically political publication. It is followed by *Magyar Hírlap* (right-wing) and *Népszava* (left-wing). Neither of these readerships exceed 5%. In 2018, 56% of the respondents reported that they do not read printed press and for those who do read *Blikk* is seen as the most credible source of information. It is followed by *HVG*, *Népszava* and *Story*. However, it must be pointed out that even *Blikk*, with its high credibility rating, does not reach 10% on this scale. This fact shows that there is a serious credibility issue in the printed press market.

Blikk has the highest number of readers, identifying it as the least credible paper. It is followed by the *Bors*, *Story* and *Lokál* trio. In other words, most people believe it as a sensational paper that is the least credible. We created a credibility scale on the basis of the reactions to the question about the most and the least credible examples of the printed press. Thus, *HVG* is the most credible magazine (6.1%). It means that the number of those who find it the most credible is 6.1% higher than the number of those who find it the least credible. It is followed by *Népszava*, *Szabad Föld* (rural right-wing) and *Magyar Hírlap*. The publications behind these have a negative credibility measure; in other words, more people believe they are the least credible than those who think they are the most credible.

News programs

The news program RTL Klub (independent, opposition) has the highest rating (61%). It is followed by TV2 Tények (pro-government) (53%), the news programs of the state-owned television (38%), the same show of Duna Television (right leaning state-funded broadcaster) (23%) and ATV (left-wing, opposition) (17%). Slightly more than one-fifth (22%) of the respondents indicated that they do not watch television because of the news programs. RTL Klub news is thought to be the least reliable news program, followed by the similar shows of TV2, ATV and M1 (right leaning state-funded broadcaster).

As with newspapers, magazines and journals, we have created a credibility measure for news programs. This shows that M1 is considered the most credible news program. 15% more people believe that it is credible than the number of those who think it is the least credible. A positive value was measured in the case of Hír TV (right-wing, pro-government), RTL Klub, CNN, Duna Tv and TV2, too (Figure 4.3).

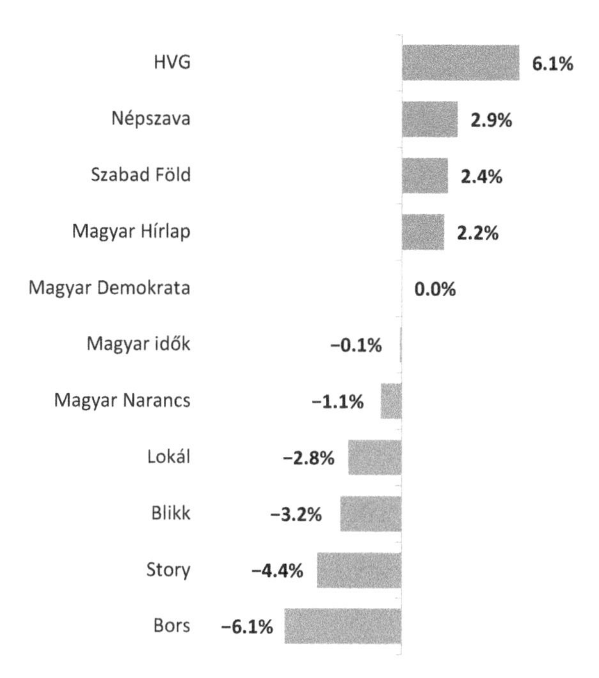

Figure 4.3 Credibility rating (printed press)

ATV and Echo TV (right-wing, pro-government) are thought to broadcast the least credible news programs. It is surprising that the credibility measure of M2 (right leaning state-funded broadcaster) shows a negative value because the news that is released there is identical to the news contents of M1, which has just been identified as the provider of the most credible news programs, despite the fact that they are government owned. The reason for this is probably that the two channels have quite different target audiences and, as a consequence, these two groups of viewers assess the same news program quite differently.

Websites

Two websites, Index (independent, opposition) and Origo (right-wing, pro-government), are the most noteworthy political websites, with nearly one-quarter of Hungarian society reading them. They are followed by 24.hu (independent, opposition), HVG Online (liberal, opposition) and 444.hu (liberal, opposition), with less than 10% of readers choosing any of the remaining websites. The most credible websites have a similar ranking. Index and Origo stand out, and they are followed by 24.hu and HVG. 888.hu (right-wing, pro-government) is at the top of

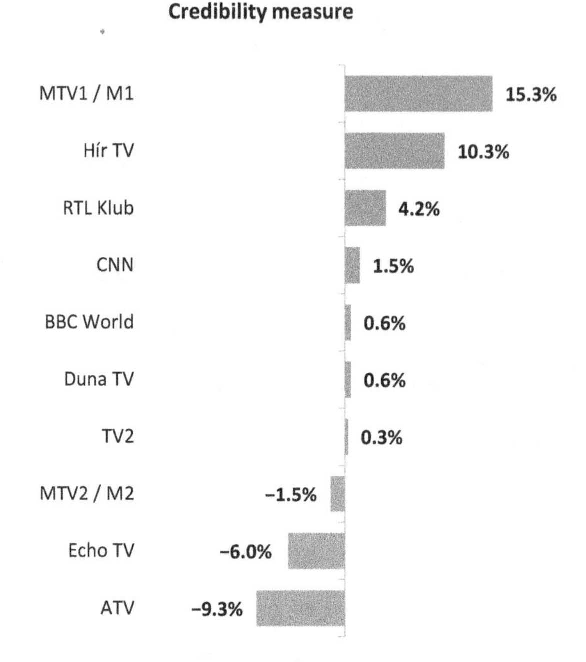

Figure 4.4 Credibility measure (news programs)

the list of the least credible websites, followed by Index, Origo and Story Online. The associated values are quite low, which shows that the market is rather fragmented in this respect, different people find different websites unreliable. Again, we used the credibility measure to get an accurate estimate. Only the most popular websites have a positive value, whereas the least credible websites include 888.hu, Story Online and kuruc.hu (far-right) (Figure 4.4).

Internet usage

As we have seen, political websites are important sources of information. It is important for us to know how much time the respondents spend online. In exploring this, we distinguish between business and non-business uses and between weekdays and weekends. 24% of the respondents use the internet on weekdays for business purposes. They spend about 3.2 hours online per day. 47% of the respondents use the internet on weekdays for non-business purposes. They spend about 2 hours online per day. 10% of the respondents use the internet on weekends for business purposes. They spend about 2.5 hours online per day. Half of the respondents use the internet on weekends for non-business purposes. They spend about 2.6 hours online per day (Figure 4.5).

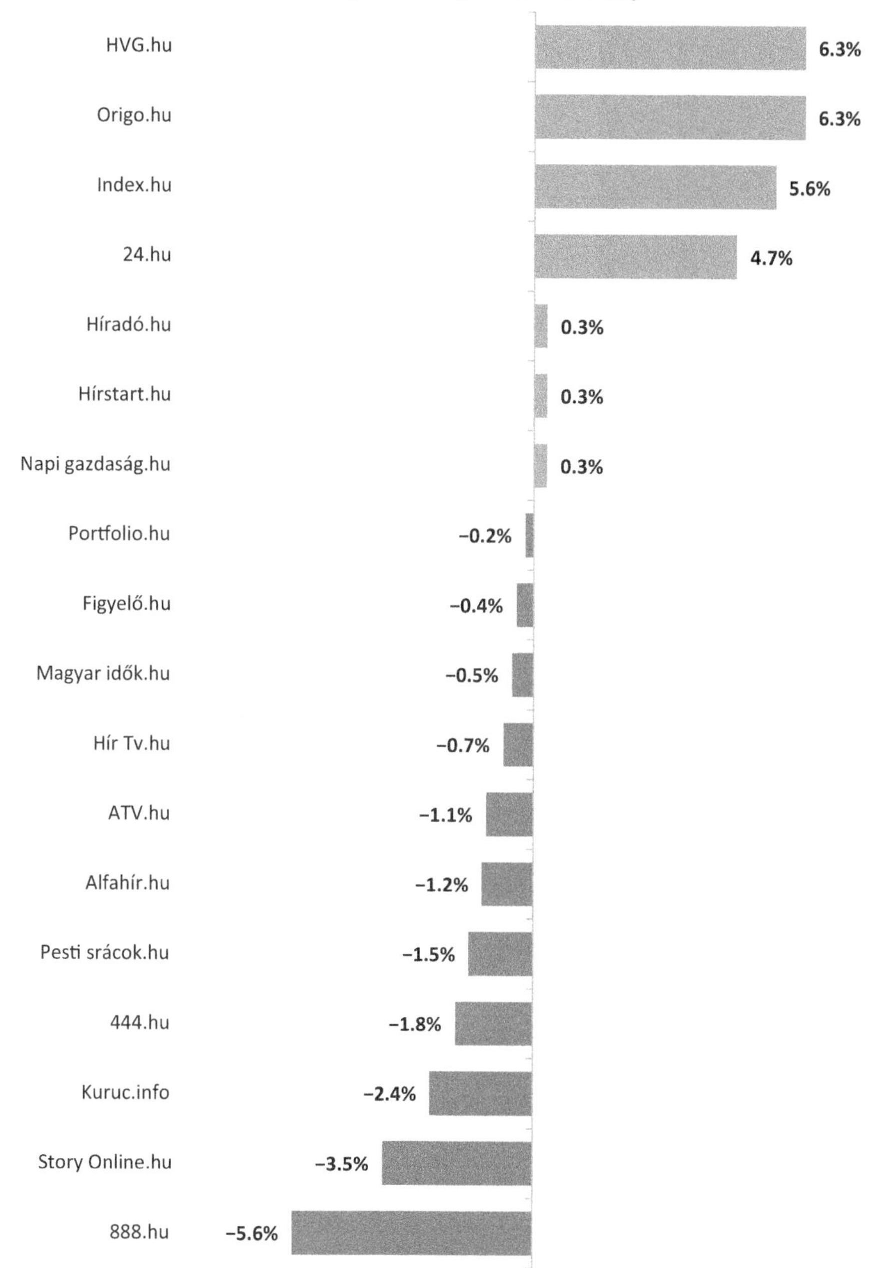

Figure 4.5 Credibility measure (political websites)

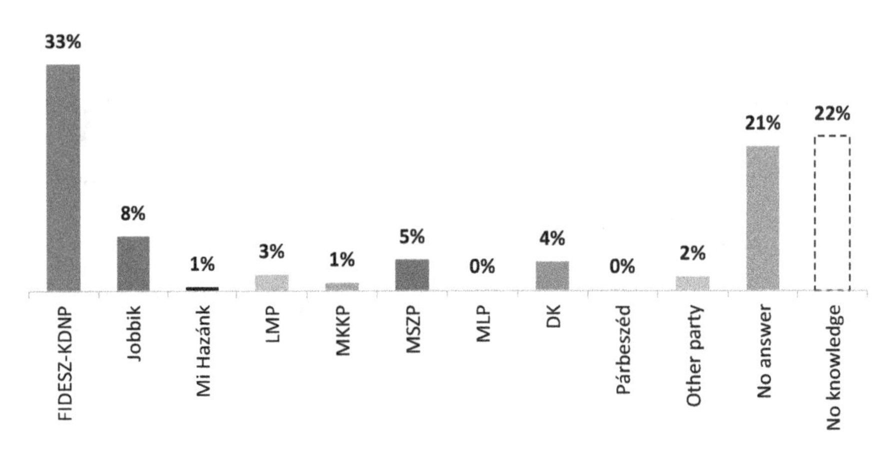

Figure 4.6 Party preferences

4.4 Party preferences

Surveying party preferences reveals that Fidesz-KDNP is the most popular party, backed by 33% of the respondents. This coalition is followed by the far-right Jobbik (8%) and MSZP (5%) and then, even further behind, the left-wing DK and LMP. 21% of the respondents did not wish to talk about their party preferences, and 22% of them were unsure how they would cast their votes if elections were held next week (Figure 4.6).

During the previous elections, 37% of the respondents voted for Fidesz-KDNP, 12% for Jobbik, 6% for MSZP and 33% for LMP and DK. 29% of the participants in the sample refused to reveal their earlier choice of a political party, and 7% were unable to remember it. In addition to data showing support, another very interesting measure is the rejection of political parties. Currently, the most clearly rejected party is Fidesz-KDNP: 35% of the respondents would not vote for this party, which is also the most popular one. This indicates that Fidesz-KDNP is the most divisive party in Hungary, followed by Jobbik, MSZP and DK, with a nearly 20% rate of rejection. In the case of the other parties, this does not reach 10%. 20% of the respondents were not willing to indicate which party they reject wholeheartedly.

Note

1 This term is comparable to, although not entirely identical with, state capitals in the USA or county towns in the UK. Hungary consists of counties with one central town or city, with its own mayoral government and administration: Veszprém is, for example, the regional capital of Veszprém County (*megye*). But this is not to imply that Hungary is a federation of states in the manner of the US.

5 Individual and society

5.1 Distribution and expectations

Findings from the 2018 data collection

94% of the Hungarian population believe that income reflects one's contribution to society, while 78% believe that a higher income should also entail a higher tax burden, which is not currently the case in Hungary. Whether or not wealth should be distributed equally is a question that divides Hungarian society, with 47% being in favor of distributing wealth equally regardless of individual contribution, while fewer people support the idea of flat rate taxation. We can see that Hungarian society is divided on this issue and, confusingly, some people opted for both versions of taxation (Figure 5.1).

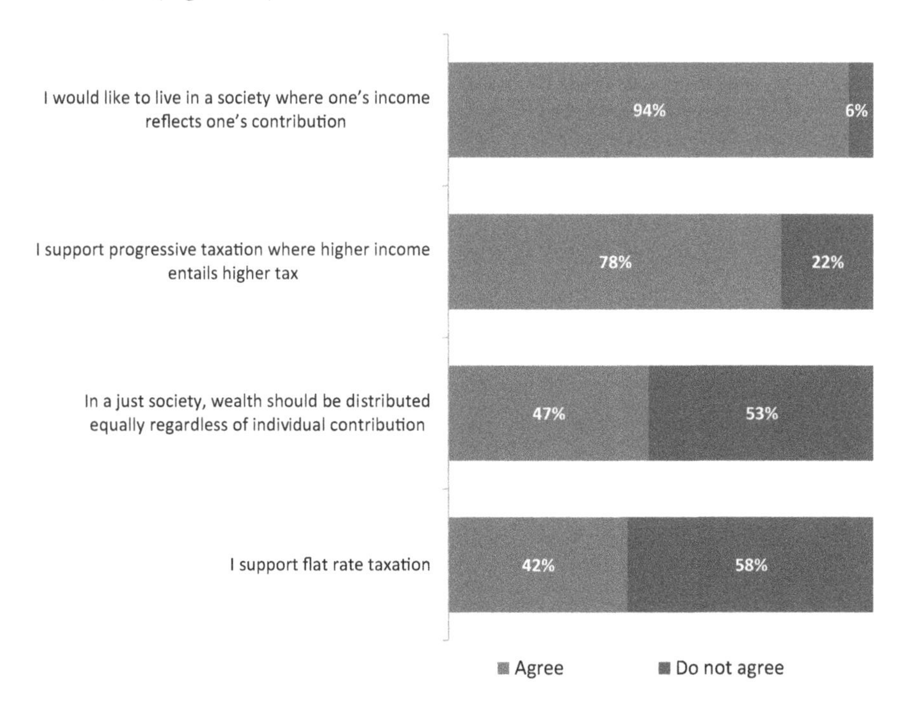

Figure 5.1 Principles of distribution

88% of the respondents believe that it is possible to make friends in today's world. 28% reported feeling lonely. But despite this, 69% feel they do not know who they can count on these days. 72% think the average person is financially worse off now. 60% believe that individuals cannot shape the world and that public administration is of little help. Another 60% find that the end justifies the means. We get a more positive picture when it comes to the desire to have a child and the meaning of life. Those who believe there is no point in having a child and life is meaningless represent a minority (Figure 5.2).

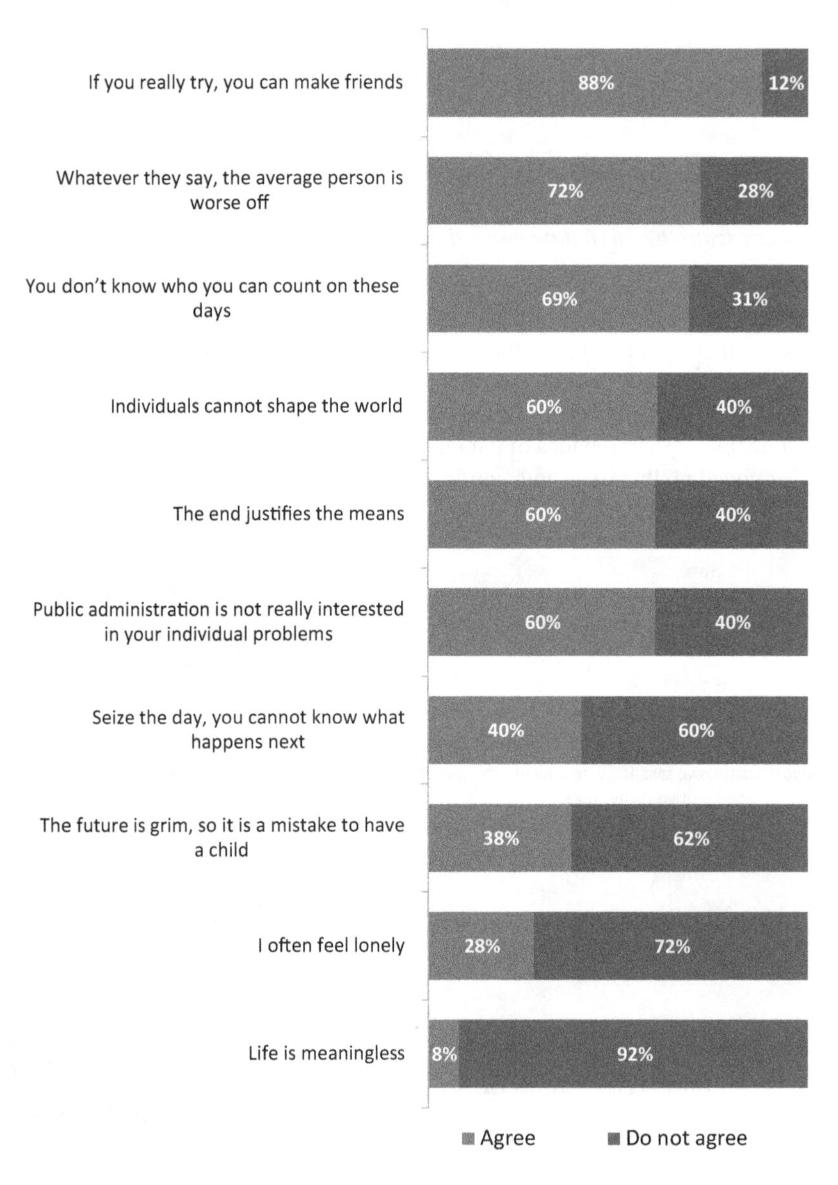

Figure 5.2 Attitudes toward the world

Multidimensional correlations

To have one's income reflect one's contribution to society is an idea with which residents in all settlement types agree, though somewhat fewer people agree with it in the capital city.[1] Residents in Budapest and the smallest settlements have the greatest support for the concept of flat rate taxation. It is important to note that people with a preference for this kind of taxation constitute a majority in Budapest (58%) in 2018.[2] Progressive taxation has the strongest base in towns and regional capitals, and even though its support is the lowest in Budapest, those in favor of it are above two-thirds of the respondents even here.[3]

Progressive taxation has the least support among the wealthiest and the poorest segments of society. It is understandable in the case of the wealthy; in the case of the underprivileged, party preference explains this choice: this social group mainly supports Fidesz, whose political agenda favors flat rate taxation.[4] Respondents with a better educational background are more likely to believe that their individual action can have meaningful impact on the world. It is people with very little education who are convinced that their actions cannot shape the world at all.[5] The most pessimistic responses came from residents of regional capitals and villages.[6]

Income is another strong factor behind faith in the power of individual action. People with a lower income are less likely to believe they have any influence, and 87% of those with the lowest income find their individual action meaningless.[7] An overwhelming majority of the respondents thinks that life is meaningful; however, about one-quarter of those who have only minimum education find that life is meaningless.[8] People in difficult financial situations cannot maintain a positive attitude toward life in general. 23% of them consider life meaningless. Among individuals with a good financial background, the same rate is only 2%.[9]

The concept that the end justifies the means divides people with higher education to the greatest extent. Among these respondents, only every third person agreed with this idea, while in groups with different educational backgrounds, this rate is above 60%.[10]

Significant differences in settlement types exist. Residents in Budapest and towns are less likely to agree with this concept, whereas residents in regional capitals and villages are more likely to endorse it.[11] Making new friends is not a problem among people with higher education; the lower one's education is, the more difficult it is to make friends.[12] Financial insecurity has a negative influence on one's capacity to form and maintain interpersonal relationships. The worse off people are, the more difficult they find it to make friends.[13]

Loneliness typically kicks in above the age of 60; the causes include problems of aging and loss of spouses and friends. In younger age groups, every fourth person reported feeling lonely. It seems that below 60, there is no correlation between age and loneliness.[14] Loneliness hits people with the lowest education the hardest (43%). This may have to do with age, because the oldest respondents were likely to have little education. Conversely, participants with a more solid educational background are less likely to feel isolated.[15] Interestingly, while about one-third of the wealthiest respondents feel lonely, only among participants in difficult financial situations is this felt by a majority (58%).[16]

The majority of respondents, regardless of their own status, believe that ordinary people are worse off than before. This opinion has the highest representation among participants with the lowest education (96%).[17] The fact that making a decent living is increasingly difficult is experienced primarily by residents in villages and regional capitals, where more than 70% of the respondents are of this opinion.[18] As can be expected, those with poor financial backgrounds are more likely to find that ordinary people are worse off than before. In this group, almost all respondents think so, while in the group of the wealthiest participants, about two-thirds of the respondents share this view.[19] Financial situation also has an impact on whether the respondents choose to have children. Participants in a difficult financial situation think it is irresponsible to have children in a climate of uncertainty. Even among the wealthiest respondents, approximately one-third believe that choosing to have a child is an irresponsible decision,[20] despite the financial incentives in the form of tax breaks from the Fidesz government, which became greater in the period studied.

55% of the participants with the lowest education think it is better to live like there is no tomorrow, whereas 24% of university graduates share this view, so planning correlates with educational background.[21] Looking at the participants' financial background, one finds that those with a more solid background are likely to plan ahead of time, whereas those with very limited means live for the present only.[22] Loss of trust is more characteristic of villages and regional capitals than of town and city dwellers.[23] 87% of the respondents in difficult financial situations reported not knowing who they can count on. This rate decreases with better finances, and it is 59% among the wealthiest respondents.[24]

Less educated respondents have lost almost all faith in public administration, and it is only among college graduates, where the majority believes it is a good idea to turn to these institutions.[25] Lack of trust in public administration is particularly characteristic of residents in regional capitals and villages, where nearly two-thirds of the respondents believed there is no point in turning to public administration.[26] Financial problems can contribute to loss of trust in public administration. 87% of those who are in the worst situation believe there is no point in turning to public administration. 55–56% of the wealthiest respondents share this view.[27]

5.2 Social problems and globalization

Findings from the 2018 data collection

Environmental pollution is in the first place. 93% of the respondents chose this issue. 92% of them think global warming the biggest challange facing us, followed by terrorism, social inequalities, migration and new epidemics. Each of these choices has support above 80%. 71% think that the clash of civilizations is a key issue, while 61% believe that bringing war criminals to justice is a priority (Figure 5.3).

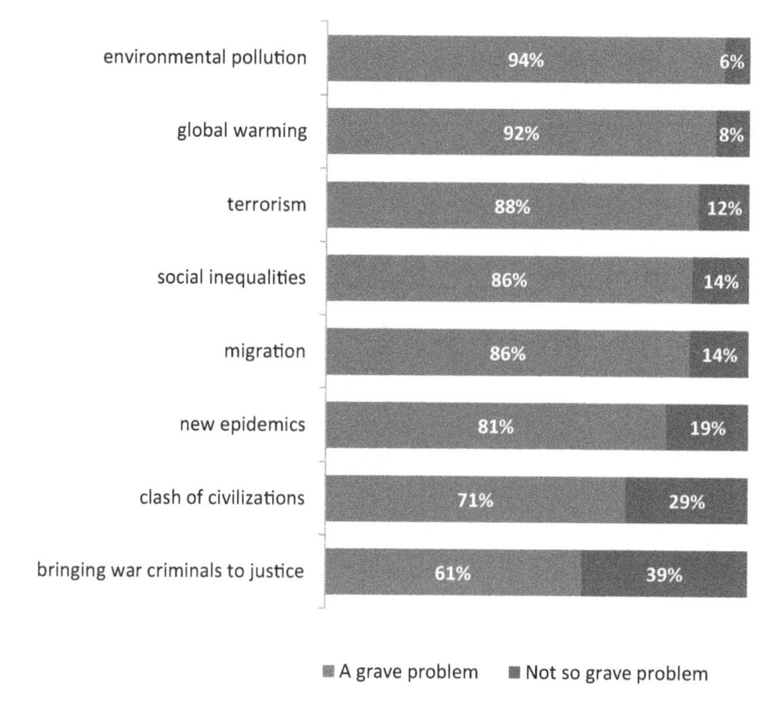

Figure 5.3 Social and environmental problems

When it comes to migration and globalization, most respondents believe that the Hungarian way of life should be protected from foreign influences. 80% of the respondents think the rights of foreigners should be curtailed to a higher extent, and 79% find that the settlement of foreigners in Hungary risks a higher crime rate. The majority argue that free movement and the right to choose one's residence are not beneficial for society. 46% believe that the development of international cooperation yields global benefit. Similarly, 43% find that cohabitation with people from diverse backgrounds leads to a more colourful life.

Multidimensional correlations

Environmental and social problems

Respondents living in larger settlements are afraid of new epidemics, whereas village dwellers are less afraid. This can be put down to the higher age of the average villager and the peculiarities of the flow of information.[28] Respondents in difficult financial situations are more likely to be afraid of epidemics.[29] Terrorism is most feared in the capital city. This fear decreases with the smaller size of a given settlement (Figure 5.4).[30]

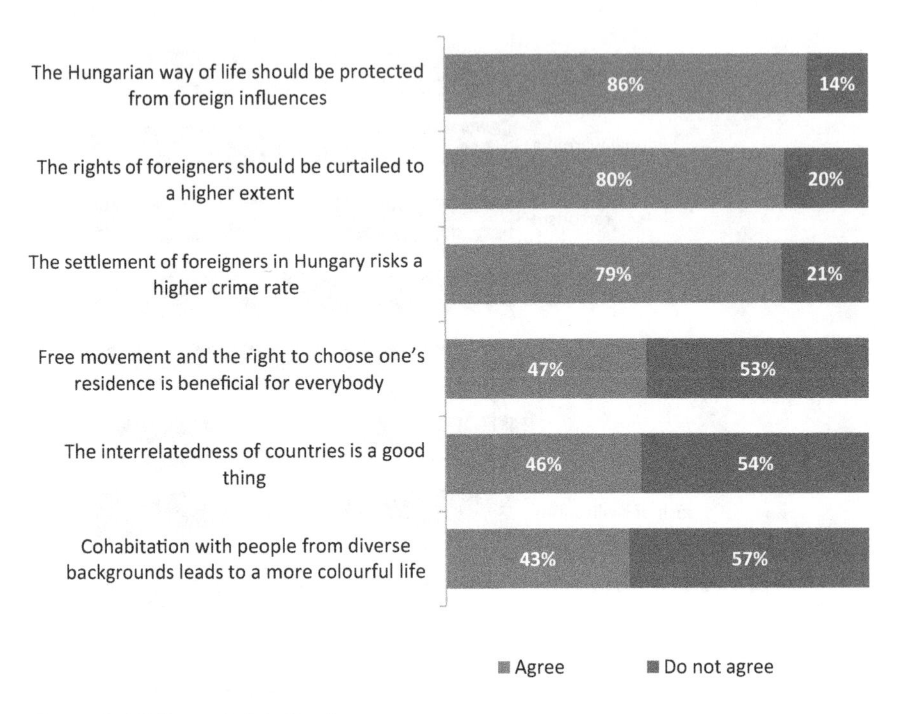

Figure 5.4 Effects of globalization

The respondents' financial situation also influences the extent to which they find terrorism to be a threat. Those in the best and the worst situations are less likely to find it a serious threat, but among them, more than 80% feel threatened.[31] Better education generates more receptivity to environmental issues in Hungarian society. All of the best-educated respondents consider environmental pollution a major problem.[32] In the capital city, 78% find that social inequalities are a serious problem, while in villages, this rate is 89%.[33] Bringing war criminals to justice is a priority, mainly for respondents in the largest settlements. Only a small majority share this view in towns and villages.[34] It is in Budapest that respondents are the most critical of the clash of different cultures (86%). The same phenomenon has the disapproval of two-thirds of the population of towns and villages.[35] Similarly, it is in Budapest that the highest rate of respondents sees migration as a major problem (91%). The smaller a settlement is, the more limited this fear is. However, even in villages, 85% of the residents fear migration.[36] This could perhaps be partly attributed to omnipresence of this issue in the state media.

Effects of globalization

It is respondents with the least education who find the idea of protection against foreign influences the most attractive (96%). This rate declines with more solid education, but even among the best-educated participants, it has an approval rate of 71%.[37] It is in Budapest that the highest number of respondents endorse the idea that the Hungarian way of life must be protected against foreign influences. This rate is the lowest in regional capitals, and it is again quite popular with town dwellers and villagers.[38] Openness toward people who are different mostly characterises the youngest respondents. In this age group, these participants constitute a majority. In other age groups, this rate is below 50%, and it decreases with older age.[39] Perhaps surprisingly, residents in towns and regional capitals are the most open, while residents in Budapest and villages tend to be closed.[40] When it comes to curtailing the rights of foreigners, respondents without higher education are more likely to endorse this idea than their better-educated peers. There is a significant difference between these two groups. More than 80% of respondents with basic education only support this idea, but among better-educated participants, it is only two-thirds.[41] The concept of curtailing foreigners' rights is more popular in villages and Budapest, and it has a more limited base in towns and regional capitals.[42] Poorly educated respondents have the least support for globalization. Only 30% find globalization is a positive phenomenon. This rate increases with better education, so among university graduates, it reaches 68%.[43]

53% of town dwellers consider the interrelatedness of countries a positive phenomenon. In other settlement types, this rate is just slightly above 40%.[44] A large percentage of respondents in Budapest (89%) think that the presence of foreigners runs the risk of a higher crime rate. This percentage drops to 73% in regional capitals.[45] Better education entails increased openness to a free and diverse world. 74% of the best-educated respondents believe that greater mobility is beneficial for everybody. Among participants with minimal education, the same rate is only 39%.[46] 63% of the best-educated respondents are in favor of freedom of movement and of residence. Only 26% of the poorest participants support the same idea.[47]

5.3 Individual and self-reflection

Findings from the 2018 data collection

A majority (84%) of the respondents are happy with themselves. 78% claim they have never offended anybody intentionally. 43% would like to have higher self-esteem. 44% report being envious of others. Only one-quarter of the respondents say there are many things they can be proud of. Every fifth respondent feels useless sometimes (Figure 5.5).

Three-quarters of the respondents enjoy tasks that permit new solutions. A small majority report they often think about problems that do not affect them directly. A more or less identical number of respondents say, however, that for them it is enough if something works fine, so they do not think about the how and the why. 38% claim they like to think about abstract issues, and the same percentage prefers to avoid situations which require a lot of thinking (Figure 5.6).

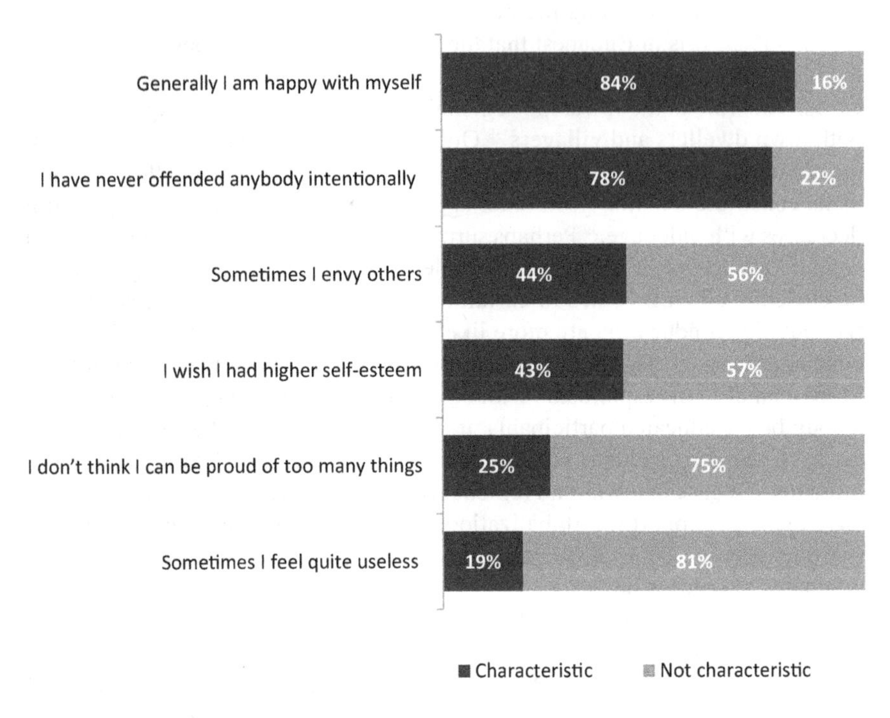

Figure 5.5 Self-reflexive attitudes

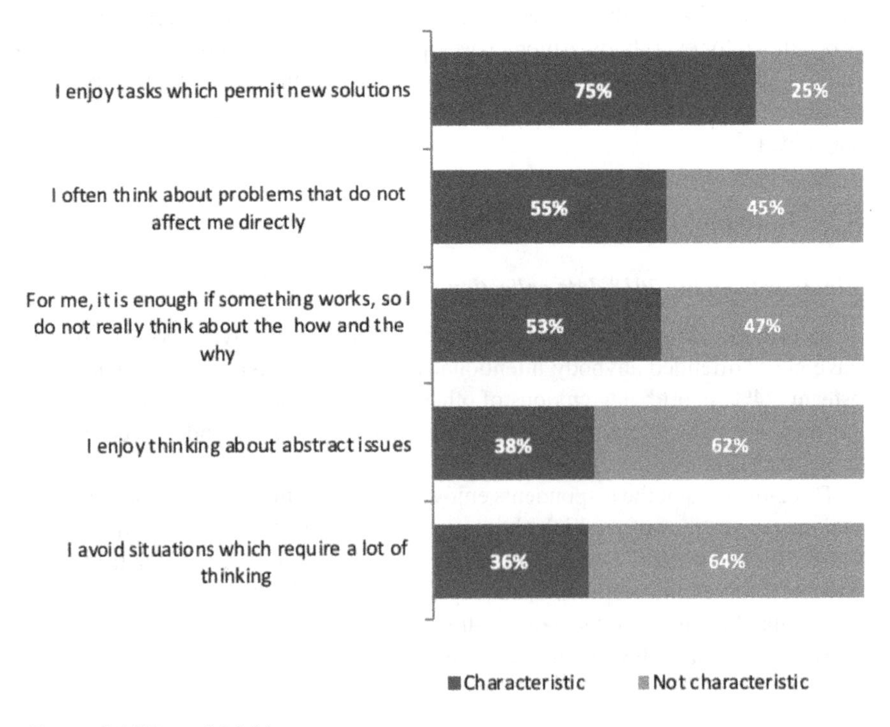

Figure 5.6 Ways of thinking

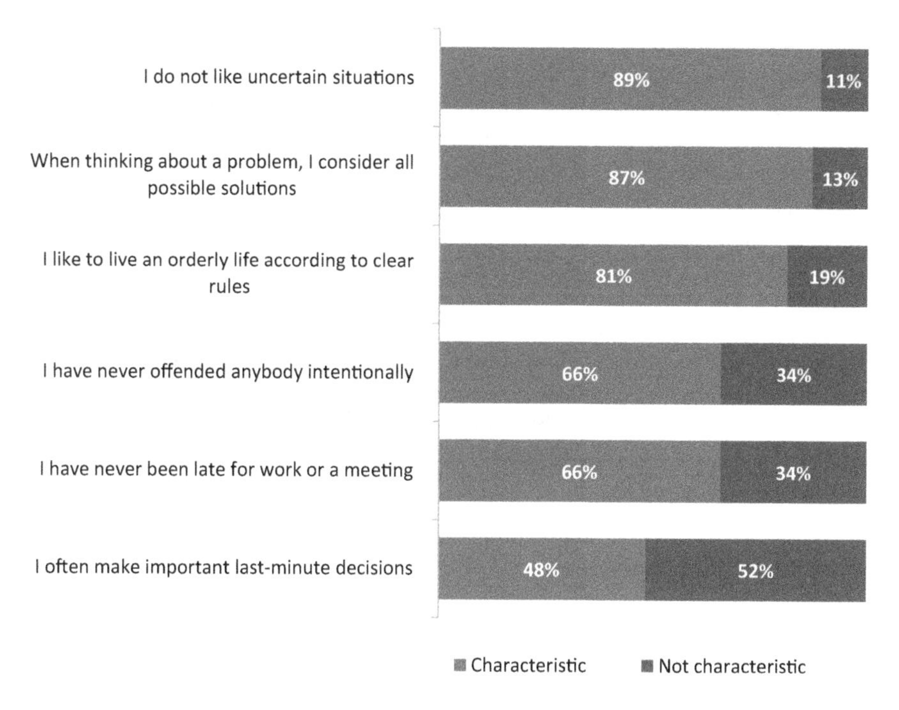

Figure 5.7 Self-characterization

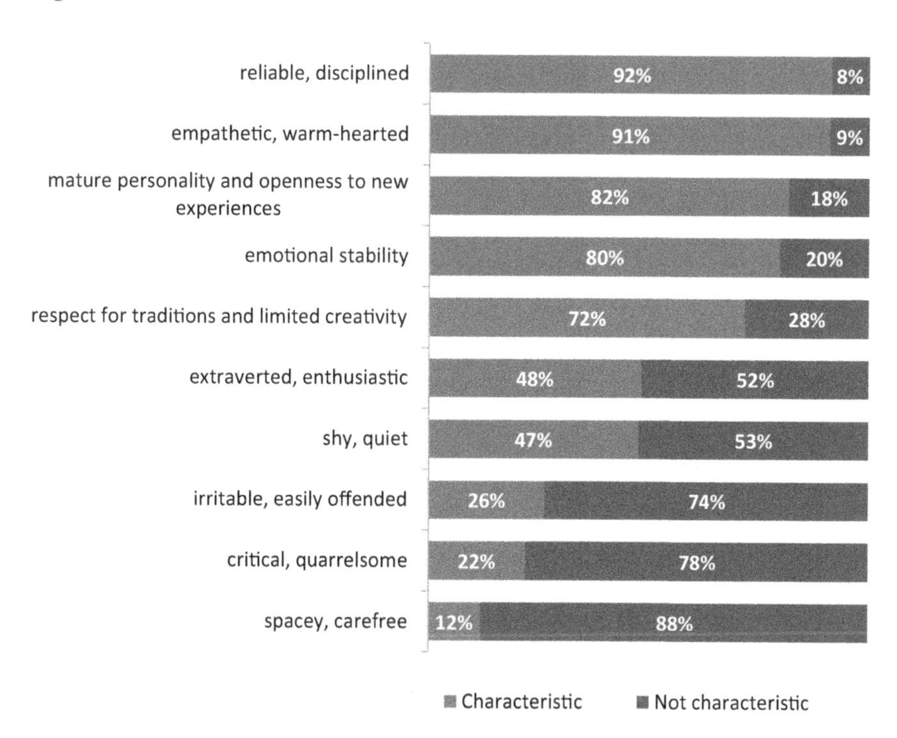

Figure 5.8 Personality traits

89% of the respondents say they do not like uncertain situations, while 87% state they consider all possible solutions when it comes to problem-solving. A large majority (81%) claim they prefer to live an orderly life in accordance with clear rules. Two-thirds of the respondents say they have never offended anybody intentionally. The same number of the participants alleges they have never been late for work. Again, about two-thirds report making last minute decisions; the same rate of the respondents say they never leave decisions to the last minute (Figure 5.7).

More than 90% of the respondents consider themselves reliable, disciplined, empathetic and warm-hearted. More than 80% believe they have a mature and emotionally stable personality and that they are open to new experiences. 72% claim to respect traditions and not have too much creativity. Extraverted, enthusiastic, shy and quiet respondents constitute a minority. Only one-quarter of the participants find they are irritable and easily offended. Every fifth person thinks he or she is too critical, even quarrelsome. A mere 12% see themselves as spacey and carefree (Figure 5.8).

Multidimensional correlations

Attitudes toward oneself

92% of the better-off respondents are happy with themselves, but as we move toward more limited finances, this rate declines. Among the poorest participants, this is only 48%.[48]

57% of the respondents with the most basic education do not think there are too many things they can be proud of. Among participants with higher qualifications, this rate is only 25%.[49] Financial difficulties have a significant impact on one's capability to think of oneself proudly. 48% of those with serious financial difficulties find it hard to think of themselves with a sense of pride. Among the wealthiest respondents, this rate is 19%.[50]

One-third of the respondents with the least education feel useless in certain situations. This rate declines with more education, so among people with college degrees, it is only 11%. However, the rate is again high, 21%, among respondents with postgraduate qualifications.[51]

Finances often determine whether one feels useless. Those with limited means are more likely to perceive themselves as useless (45%), while those who are financially comfortable are less likely to see themselves in that light (17%).[52]

81% of the female respondents claim they have never offended anybody intentionally. Among male participants, this rate is 75%.[53] Those who think they have never offended anybody intentionally are fewer in number in regional capitals than elsewhere. In other settlement types, this rate is around 80%.[54] The rate of those who claim they have never offended anybody intentionally is higher among wealthier respondents than among their less affluent peers.[55] 61% of the least educated respondents would like to have higher self-esteem. This rate declines with more education; however, it is again high among the best-educated respondents (47%).[56]

Near half of those with more limited finances would like to have higher self-esteem; this rate declines to 35% among the most affluent respondents.[57] It is the youngest respondents who are the most eager to have higher self-esteem (68%). With age, this rate declines, and among the eldest participants, it is only 33%.[58]

Ways of thinking

Respondents with the least education are quite likely to avoid situations requiring a lot of thought. Among them, this rate is 74%, but with more education, it declines, and among university graduates, it drops to 12%.[59] Those with poor finances tend to avoid situations requiring a lot of thinking (68%); but with a better financial background, this avoidance becomes less pronounced (31%).[60]

A higher rate of men than women reported enjoying situations that call for new solutions.[61] To be interested in new solutions is more typical of better-educated respondents and less typical of participants with only basic education. Among respondents who did not finish primary school, only 61% are open to such challenges.[62] Compared to other settlement types, residents in regional capitals are less likely to enjoy situations that call for new solutions. Elsewhere, this ratio is more or less identical.[63] A higher rate (83%) of respondents with a comfortable financial background reported enjoying situations that call for new solutions. With a less stable background, this rate declines and reaches 48% among the poorest participants.[64] Young respondents are much more likely to enjoy thinking about abstract issues than their older peers. 55% of them expressed this preference, while among the eldest participants, the same rate is only 27%.[65]

Better education entails the readiness to think in an abstract manner. The higher level one's education is, the more probable this way of thinking is.[66] The desire to understand how things work is more characteristic of men than women. Among male respondents, 57% would like to have a better understanding of how things work, while among their female peers, this rate is 41%.[67] Not to explore causes behind things is typical of less educated participants. 74% of individuals with the least education share this attitude, and with higher levels of education, this rate declines until it hits only 26% among university graduates.[68] Education and financial background are interrelated, so it is no surprise that respondents with poor finances are less likely to explore causes behind things than their better-educated peers.[69] A higher rate of respondents in better-educated groups think about problems that do not affect them directly than in groups with less education. In the latter category, those who do not usually think about such questions constitute a majority.[70] As suggested earlier, education and financial background are connected. For this reason, affluent respondents think about problems that do not affect them personally more frequently than participants with limited means.[71]

Self-characterization

91% of female and 86% of male respondents dislike uncertain situations.[72] Disliking uncertain situations is more typical of older people than younger ones. Only among the youngest participants, this rate is below 80% (74%).[73] Regional capitals have the lowest rate of those who do not like uncertain situations (82%).[74] The better educated a respondent is, the more likely he or she is to think in a complex manner and to consider a larger selection of possibilities.[75] It is in Budapest and in the smallest settlements that the highest number of residents look at a large selection of possible solutions to a given problem. 90% of the respondents think in this way, while in regional capitals, this rate is 81%.[76] Stronger financial backgrounds make respondents more likely to consider a large number of possible solutions when it comes to problem-solving. A lower rate of participants with limited finances resorts to this strategy.[77] Half of all younger people reported being regularly late for work, while in the older age group, it is more likely to find someone who has never been late for work.[78]

84% of women prefer to live an orderly life, a slightly lower rate (78%) of men report the same.[79] With age, more and more respondents require an orderly and regulated life. Those who do not necessarily insist on such sense of order can be found mainly in the younger age groups.[80] It is primarily residents in Budapest and villages who appreciate living an orderly life in accordance with clear rules. Only 73% of residents in regional capitals share this sentiment.[81] The rate of those who make important last-minute decisions is higher among men (52%, a majority) than among women (45%).[82] Because it has been established that elderly people are quite likely to prefer living an orderly, regulated life, it follows that they are also keen to avoid situations where they have to make last minute decisions. While 74% of young respondents make important last minute decisions, the same rate is only 30% in the eldest age group.[83] Hurting the feelings of others is mainly associated with younger respondents (47%). With age, this rate declines, so 75% of the oldest participants claim they have never offended anybody.[84]

Personality traits

85% of the youngest respondents see themselves as extraverted and enthusiastic, and among the eldest participants, this rate drops to 35%.[85] 56% of the best-educated respondents see themselves as extraverted, and among those who finished less than eight grades in school, this rate is only 27%.[86] There is a higher rate of those who see themselves as extraverted and enthusiastic among respondents with stable financial backgrounds.[87] One-quarter of men see themselves as quarrelsome and too critical, while only one-fifth of women have the same self-image.[88]

A smaller rate of residents in Budapest and villages sees themselves as quarrelsome and too critical. In these two groups, this rate is around 20%, while in towns and regional capitals, it is nearly 25%.[89] 94% of women and 89% of men find themselves reliable and disciplined.[90] 79% of the young respondents consider themselves disciplined. This rate increases with age, and it reaches 95% among the oldest respondents.[91] No obvious correlation appears between educational background and the idea that one is reliable and disciplined. Fewer respondents with only primary school education and more with high school diplomas and university degrees have this self-image.[92] It is in regional capitals that people find themselves the least reliable, and this is just the opposite in villages and the capital city.[93]

Those struggling with serious problems often have a damaged self-image, only 67% of them see themselves as reliable and disciplined.[94] One-third of the respondents in villages think they are irritable and easily offended, while in the capital city, this rate is only 15%.[95]

One's financial situation also has an impact on one's psychological well-being. 47% of those who experience difficulties in this field see themselves as irritable and easily offended. Among affluent respondents, this rate is only 19%.[96] 89% of the youngest respondents reported being open to new experiences. This rate declines with age, and among the oldest participants, it is only 64%.[97] Being open to new experiences increases with educational background and it reaches 94%, while in the least educated group, 68% of the participants believe they have grown as a person and they are open to new experiences.[98]

Better financial situations are usually accompanied by more open personalities, so in this group the related rate is above 80%, but if these situations worsen, the same rate is closer to 70%.[99] A high rate (62%) of the oldest respondents sees themselves as shy and quiet. There is no significant difference between the other age groups in this regard, where the same rate is slightly below 50%.[100] A higher rate of residents in villages and Budapest claim they are shy and quiet than those in towns.[101] Respondents with a strong financial background are likely to believe they are calm and emotionally stable. The worse this background becomes, the fewer participants have this self-image. Among those who are in the worst financial situation, only 37% see themselves in this light.[102]

A higher rate of elderly respondents claim to respect traditions and have not too much creativity. Among them, it is 84%, while among the youngest participants, it is only 55%.[103]

Only half of those with the worst financial backgrounds think they respect traditions and that they do not have too much creativity. In the other groups, this rate is higher than 70%.[104]

5.4 People and communities

Findings from the 2018 data collection

Human nature

For an overwhelming majority of Hungarians, the existence of social hierarchies is an unquestionable fact of life. 90% of the respondents find it important

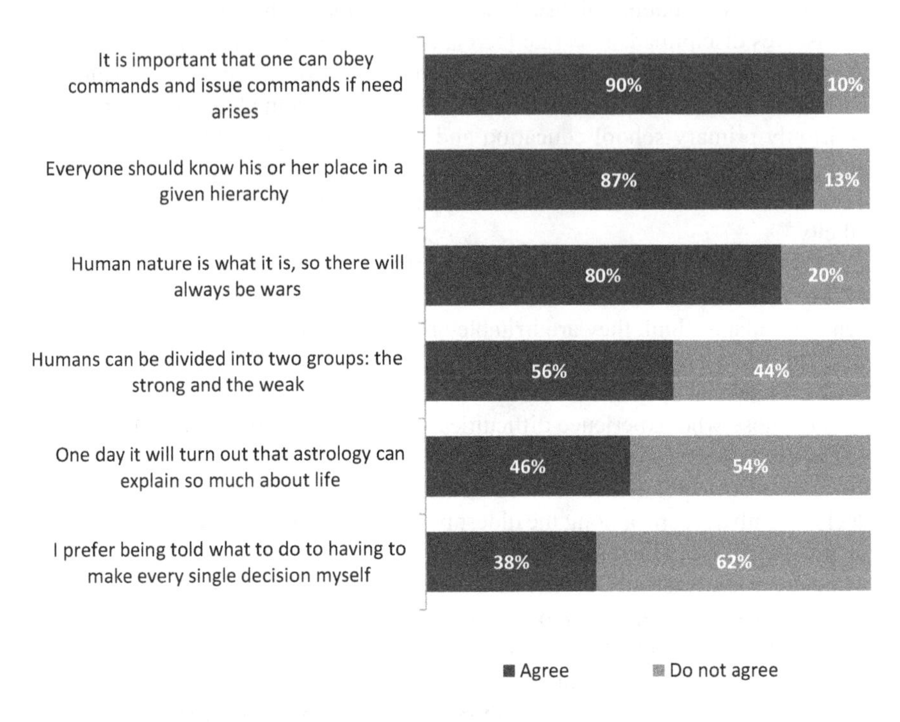

Figure 5.9 Judging human nature

that one is able to obey commands and issue commands, if the need arises; 87% believe that everyone should know his or her place in a given hierarchy. More than one-third (38%) not only accept the existence of social hierarchies, but they also prefer being told what to do because this gets rid of the responsibility of making decisions. Similarly, an overwhelming majority (86%) considers aggression a basic human instinct, claiming there will always be wars. Interestingly, these respondents are more cautious when it comes to the significance of aggression. A much smaller percentage (56%) think that power alone is a sufficient basis of comparing humans. Finally, nearly half of the respondents (46%) believe in astrology, which highlights a lack of trust in science and rationality, according to Adorno's F-Scale (Figure 5.9).

The importance of communities

What communities are important for Hungarians? Unsurprisingly, 98% of Hungarians find families to be the most important community. This is followed by the country itself, then the neighborhood, the workplace and, finally, the EU, but even this is seen as important by 74% of the respondents (Figure 5.10).

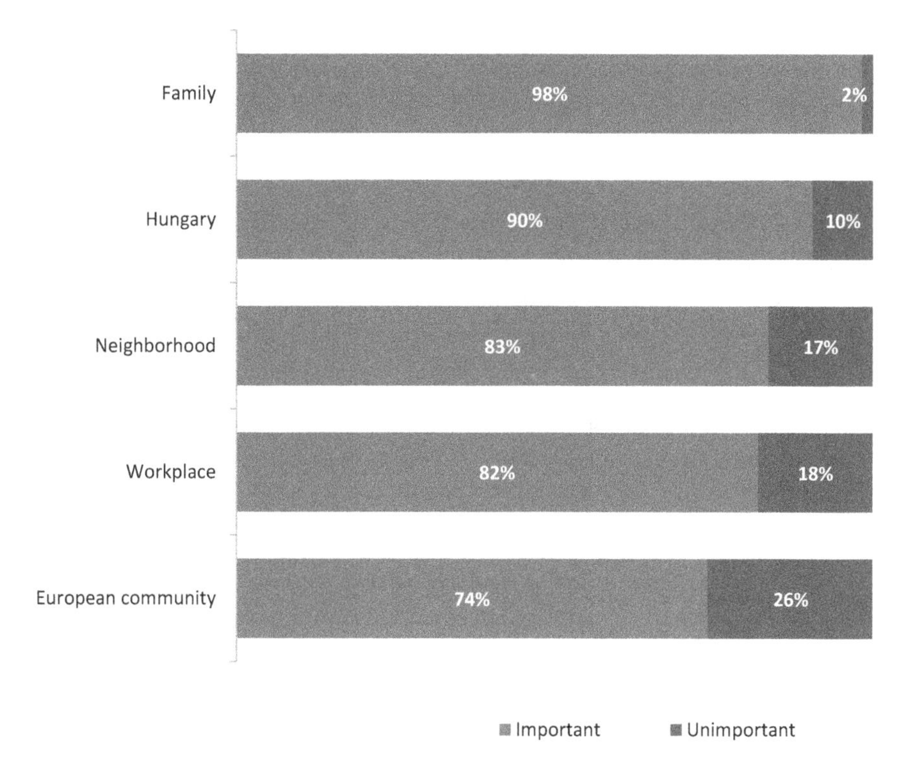

Figure 5.10 The importance of communities

Multidimensional correlations

Human nature

Respondents with comfortable financial backgrounds are more likely to feel they need to learn how to obey commands and how to issue commands, too. 94% of them share this view, while among participants with poor finances, this rate is 71%.[105] The need for independence increases with better education. Only 9% of university graduates prefer being told what to do, while among participants with minimal education, this rate is 61%.[106] In terms of settlement types, we find the lowest rate of people who prefer being told what to do in Budapest (25%). Elsewhere, the same rate is around 40%.[107] The need for independence increases along with improving finances, but interestingly, it drops to 54% among the wealthiest respondents. On the next most favorable level, it is 67%, while among respondents with the worst finances, less than half (42%) prefer independence.[108] To derive the existence of wars from human nature is the least acceptable in towns (73%); in other settlement types, this rate is above 80%.[109] More than half of women (51%)

believe in astrology, which, for Adorno, is an indication of an authoritarian mindset, while among men, this rate is only 41%.[110] Of course, a better image of whether this number is unusual could be gleaned by comparing this percentage with the immediate region and the rest of Europe, so as to ascertain whether a history of authoritarian government results in an increase in anti-scientific thought.

The importance of communities

It is the group of 30- to 39-year-olds that attribute the least importance to the role of families, but even here, it is only 5% that find this role insignificant. We assume that the highest number of those who do not yet or no longer live in families is in this group.[111] Residents in Budapest attribute the least importance to families, but even among them, 96% find families important.[112] The communal role of neighborhoods has the least value for Budapest dwellers (76%). As settlement type becomes smaller, this value increases, so among villagers, it reaches 91%.[113] A higher rate of respondents with stable finances emphasize the importance of neighborhoods. It should be noted that this group has the necessary mobility to choose or change the place of their residence.[114]

Evidently, it is middle-aged respondents who attribute the most significance to workplace communities. This has a lower value for younger and older participants, because their sense of being directly involved in such communities is weaker. They may not yet, or they may no longer, live a working life.[115] Workplace communities are the least important for residents in regional capitals and they are the most important for villagers (86%).[116] There is a correlation between the appreciation of workplace communities and the respondents' financial situation. The lowest rate to attach importance to such communities is among participants with limited means (76%). This may signal that they work under the worst circumstances. Respondents with serious financial challenges may not be employed at all; therefore, their desire to belong to a workplace community may be stronger than the memory of earlier frustrations in such places.[117] Hungary, as a community, was highly valued in all settlement types, especially in the capital city (96%) and villages (92%). This rate is slightly lower in towns (88%) and regional capitals (86%).[118]

The least importance is associated with Hungary in groups with the worst and the best financial backgrounds, but even here the rate is above 80%.[119] The appreciation of the EU increases with better education, and among the least educated respondents, 57% find the Union important as a community, but among university graduates, this rate is 85%.[120]

It seems that the European community is more important for respondents who see themselves as middle-class (91%, 92%) than for their richest and poorest peers (81%, 84%).[121]

Notes

1 khi^2=0,102 p=0,015
2 khi^2=0,165 p=0,000

3 khi^2=0,131 p=0,001
4 khi^2=0,105 p=0,012
5 khi^2=0,147 p=0,000
6 khi^2=0,124 p=0,001
7 khi^2=0,202 p=0,000
8 khi^2=0,112 p=0,014
9 khi^2=0,132 p=0,001
10 khi^2=0,101 p=0,044
11 khi^2=0,123 p=0,002
12 khi^2=0,100 p=0,040
13 khi^2=0,103 p=0,014
14 khi^2=0,132 p=0,008
15 khi^2=0,134 p=0,001
16 khi^2=0,189 p=0,000
17 khi^2=0,108 p=0,021
18 khi^2=0,145 p=0,000
19 khi^2=0,161 p=0,000
20 khi^2=0,102 p=0,016
21 khi^2=0,135 p=0,001
22 khi^2=0,155 p=0,000
23 khi^2=0,099 p=0,021
24 khi^2=0,122 p=0,002
25 khi^2=0,144 p=0,000
26 khi^2=0,105 p=0,011
27 khi^2=0,165 p=0,000
28 khi^2=0,106 p=0,011
29 khi^2=0,089 p=0,049
30 khi^2=0,097 p=0,025
31 khi^2=0,091 p=0,042
32 khi^2=0,116 p=0,009
33 khi^2=0,112 p=0,006
34 khi^2=0,159 p=0,000
35 khi^2=0,164 p=0,000
36 khi^2=0,090 p=0,045
37 khi^2=0,133 p=0,002
38 khi^2=0,171 p=0,000
39 khi^2=0,124 p=0,017
40 khi^2=0,097 p=0,024
41 khi^2=0,167 p=0,000
42 khi^2=0,142 p=0,000
43 khi^2=0,103 p=0,032
44 khi^2=0,096 p=0,027
45 khi^2=0,133 p=0,001
46 khi^2=0,157 p=0,000
47 khi^2=0,108 p=0,009
48 khi^2=0,249 p=0,000
49 khi^2=0,139 p=0,001
50 khi^2=0,160 p=0,000
51 khi^2=0,113 p=0,013
52 khi^2=0,148 p=0,000
53 khi^2=0,075 p=0,017
54 khi^2=0,093 p=0,035
55 khi^2=0,140 p=0,000
56 khi^2=0,106 p=0,024

57 khi^2=0,089 p=0,049
58 khi^2=0,139 p=0,004
59 khi^2=0,226 p=0,000
60 khi^2=0,214 p=0,000
61 khi^2=0,064 p=0,044
62 khi^2=0,156 p=0,000
63 khi^2=0,096 p=0,027
64 khi^2=0,186 p=0,000
65 khi^2=0,150 p=0,001
66 khi^2=0,146 p=0,000
67 khi^2=0,133 p=0,000
68 khi^2=0,142 p=0,000
69 khi^2=0,111 p=0,007
70 khi^2=0,146 p=0,000
71 khi^2=0,101 p=0,017
72 khi^2=0,080 p=0,011
73 khi^2=0,129 p=0,011
74 khi^2=0,115 p=0,004
75 khi^2=0,137 p=0,001
76 khi^2=0,105 p=0,012
77 khi^2=0,189 p=0,000
78 khi^2=0,164 p=0,000
79 khi^2=0,072 p=0,023
80 khi^2=0,137 p=0,005
81 khi^2=0,151 p=0,000
82 khi^2=0,064 p=0,045
83 khi^2=0,180 p=0,000
84 khi^2=0,135 p=0,006
85 khi^2=0,128 p=0,013
86 khi^2=0,111 p=0,015
87 khi^2=0,128 p=0,001
88 khi^2=0,084 p=0,008
89 khi^2=0,091 p=0,042
90 khi^2=0,103 p=0,001
91 khi^2=0,113 p=0,047
92 khi^2=0,125 p=0,004
93 khi^2=0,106 p=0,011
94 khi^2=0,183 p=0,000
95 khi^2=0,129 p=0,001
96 khi^2=0,189 p=0,000
97 khi^2=0,164 p=0,000
98 khi^2=0,143 p=0,000
99 khi^2=0,158 p=0,000
100 khi^2=0,113 p=0,049
101 khi^2=0,091 p=0,042
102 khi^2=0,226 p=0,000
103 khi^2=0,253 p=0,000
104 khi^2=0,091 p=0,043
105 khi^2=0,119 p=0,003
106 khi^2=0,187 p=0,000
107 khi^2=0,126 p=0,001
108 khi^2=0,166 p=0,000
109 khi^2=0,127 p=0,001

110 khi^2=0,101 p=0,001
111 khi^2=0,138 p=0,004
112 khi^2=0,090 p=0,045
113 khi^2=0,167 p=0,000
114 khi^2=0,170 p=0,000
115 khi^2=0,179 p=0,000
116 khi^2=0,097 p=0,025
117 khi^2=0,095 p=0,029
118 khi^2=0,113 p=0,005
119 khi^2=0,089 p=0,048
120 khi^2=0,119 p=0,007
121 khi^2=0,149 p=0,000

6 Law, crime and the justice system

6.1 Legislation, judicial practice, death penalty and the causes of crime

As earlier, we measured agreement with statements about legislation and judicial practice with the help of a four-point Likert scale. Then we converted the four-point scales into two-point ones (Agree or Do not agree), thereby creating the relevant data for our analysis.

Findings from the 2018 data collection

Legislation and judicial practice

There are two statements on the list with which most respondents agree. More than four-fifths of the respondents believe that harsher sentences can deter crime. Nearly the same number, 77%, agree with the statement that prison terms in themselves do not reduce crime. Another statement assumed that increased welfare spending can lead to less crime. This idea had the approval and disapproval of the same rate of participants. Nearly one-third of the respondents would support the legalization of marihuana, and only every fifth participant believes that abortion should be banned. The restoration of the death penalty has the approval of the small majority (54%) of society.

Attitudes toward the death penalty

We have studied attitudes toward the death penalty in depth, making an effort to disclose the less obvious motivations of the advocates and the opponents of abolition. To this end, we have formulated four statements and the respondents had to choose the one with which they identify to the greatest extent. 30% chose to support the restoration of the death penalty, claiming this is the only just punishment to fit the most serious crimes. Similarly, 24% support the restoration of the death penalty, arguing that in the case of incorrigible criminals, this is the best way to protect society (Figure 6.1).

Another group (18%) finds that the death penalty does not deter crime, and yet another, somewhat larger group (22%) argues that the state does not have the right to take anybody's life. 6% of the respondents could not identify with any of the statements (Figure 6.2).

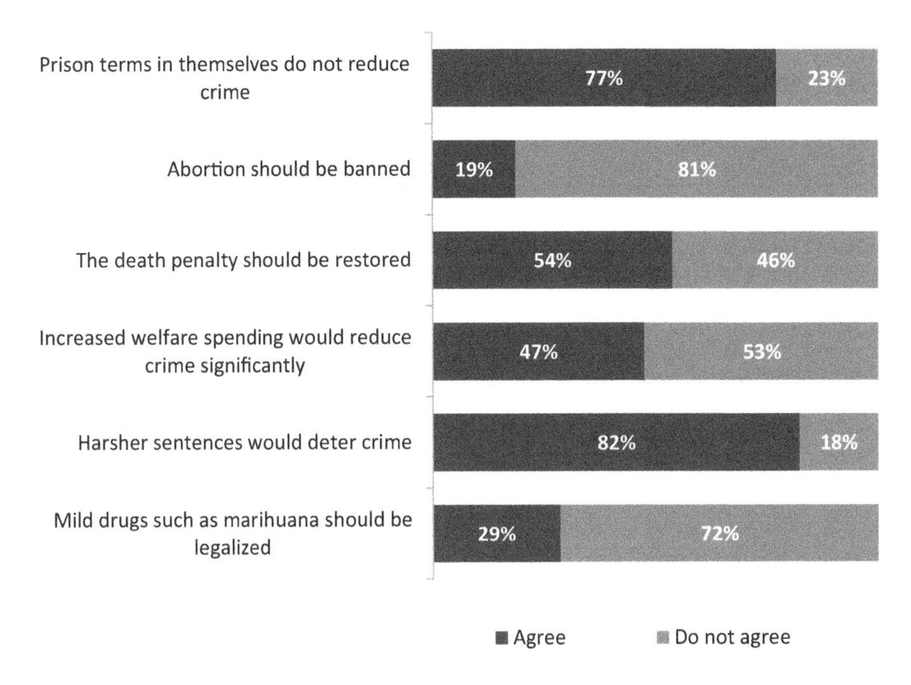

Figure 6.1 Statements about legislation and judicial practice

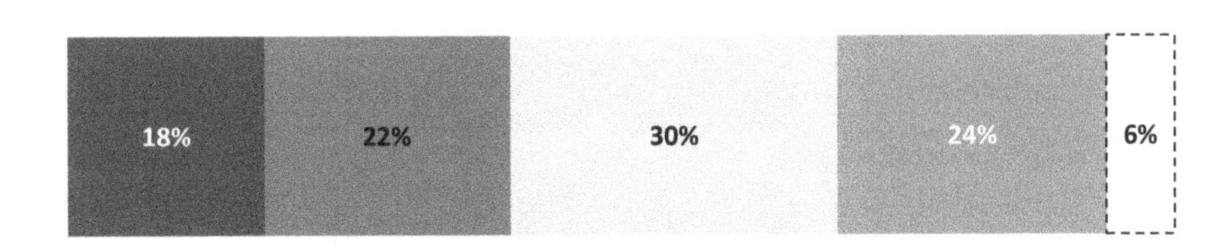

Figure 6.2 Attitudes toward the death penalty

Causes of crime decline

How do Hungarians think about the tools of crime prevention? We used the following set of items to explore how people think about factors leading to a reduced crime rate. What could be the causes of crime decline? These causes were identified through the use of the following statements.

Respondents believe that the most effective deterrents are harsher sentencing (88%) and stricter laws (87%). 79% find that tighter communities could produce a lower crime rate. Nearly two-thirds claim that more discipline in schools and full employment would lead to less crime. One half of the participants think that increased welfare spending could result in decreased crime (Figure 6.3).

Multidimensional correlations

What are the differences between social groups with regard to our list of statements? The rate of agreement and disagreement within a given socio-demographic group helps us find an answer.

Legislation and jurisdiction

It is in Budapest and towns that respondents have the strongest belief in the preventive power of increased welfare spending. In regional capitals and villages,

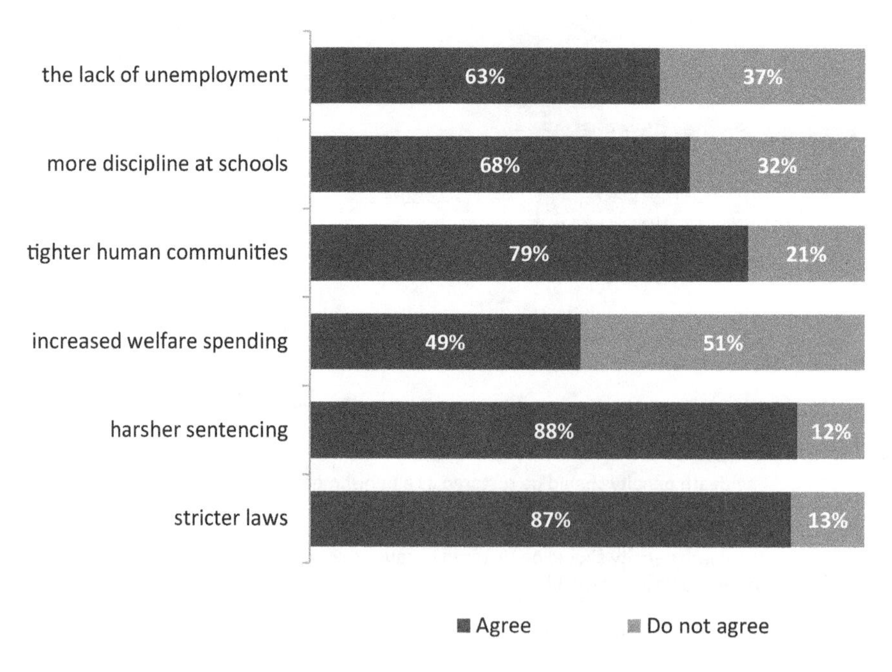

Figure 6.3 Causes of crime decline

participants are more skeptical.[1] Only town dwellers have some doubts about harsher sentencing as deterrents, but even among them, 74% have positive expectations.[2]

Two-thirds of men and one-quarter of women endorse the legalization of milder drugs.[3] Young respondents have the highest rate of support for the legalization of milder drugs (45%), and with age, this rate decreases to about 25%.[4] No clear related tendency can be observed by reference to settlement types, but it is visible that a higher rate of respondents support legalization in regional capitals than elsewhere.[5] Support for the restoration of the death penalty shows significant differences in the social groups examined. Supporters constitute a majority among men, while women are completely divided on this issue.[6] Participants with little education are more likely to support the reintroduction of capital punishment, whereas respondents with high-level education are more likely to oppose the idea.[7] Supporters represent a large majority in regional capitals and villages, and advocates and opponents are equal in number in other settlement types.[8] Within the context of subjectively perceived financial situation, one finds that a significant majority (81%) of respondents with the most serious money troubles support the reintroduction of capital punishment, whereas 56% of the participants with the best financial backgrounds oppose it.[9]

Attitudes toward the death penalty

Similarly, attitudes toward the death penalty deeply divide social groups in Hungarian society. Women are more likely to argue that the state does not have the right to take anybody's life than men, while among men a higher rate claim that the death penalty protects citizens against incorrigible criminals.[10] In terms of education, one can observe that respondents with the least schooling justify their call for the reintroduction of the capital punishment, arguing that this measure would protect society against incorrigible criminals. This argument is less popular with better-educated participants who prefer to claim that the state does not have the right to take anybody's life.[11] In terms of settlement types, one can see that the previous arguments divide participants quite markedly. A higher-than-average rate of Budapest dwellers endorse the idea that the death penalty does not deter crime. Among residents in regional capitals, the protective function of the death penalty is the key argument, whereas in towns, human life has priority over state interests. Like dwellers in regional capitals, villagers emphasize the protective function of the death penalty.[12] With regard to money, we find that the poorest respondents think that justice is the main consideration behind the restoration of the death penalty.[13]

Causes of crime decline

A high rate of town dwellers (72%) believe that the elimination of unemployment would lead to less crime. A lower rate (55%) agrees with this in villages.[14] Residents in Budapest and towns have the most trust in increased welfare spending to reduce crime. Here, they constitute a majority, while in the other two settlement types, they remain a minority.[15]

Respondents with the worst and the best finances think alike about the correlation between crime and increased welfare spending – the large majority of them believe that increased welfare spending would have a preventive function. This idea has the least support in the group whose members claim to do relatively well but within clear limits.[16] The majority of participants approve the idea that harsher sentences could lead to a lower crime rate. It is in Budapest and villages that people especially support this idea. Most disagreement can be observed in towns.[17] Harsher criminal laws have somewhat lower support in towns (81%), while elsewhere this rate is around 90%.[18] Those who claim to do relatively well but within clear financial limits have slightly less (84%) faith in the preventive function of harsher criminal code.[19]

6.2 Becoming a criminal

Findings from the 2018 data collection

Why do some people become criminals? We can see that respondents contribute the primary role to innate, subjective elements. Among the leading causes are aggressivity, one's aggressive disposition, being impulsive, greed and mental illness. Correspondingly, external factors appear at the end of the list: poverty, media violence and the lack of social stability (Figure 6.4).

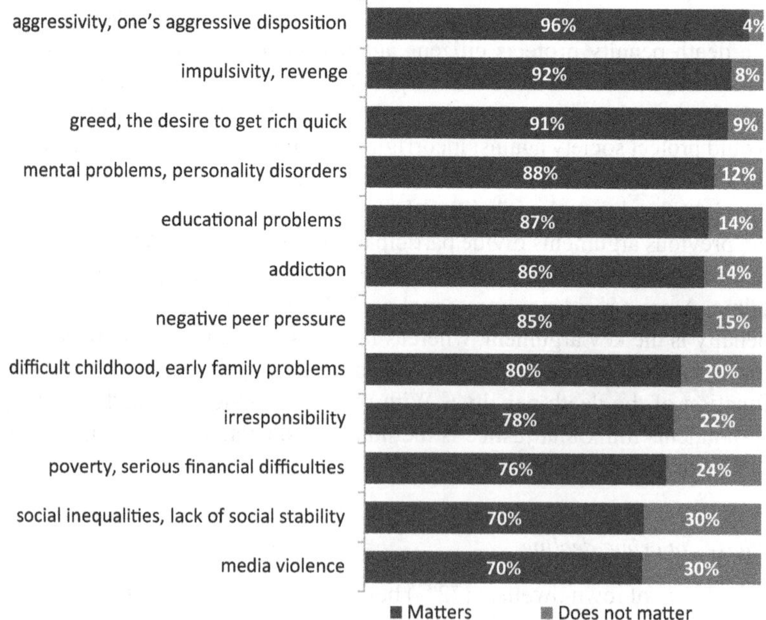

Figure 6.4 Causes of criminal behavior

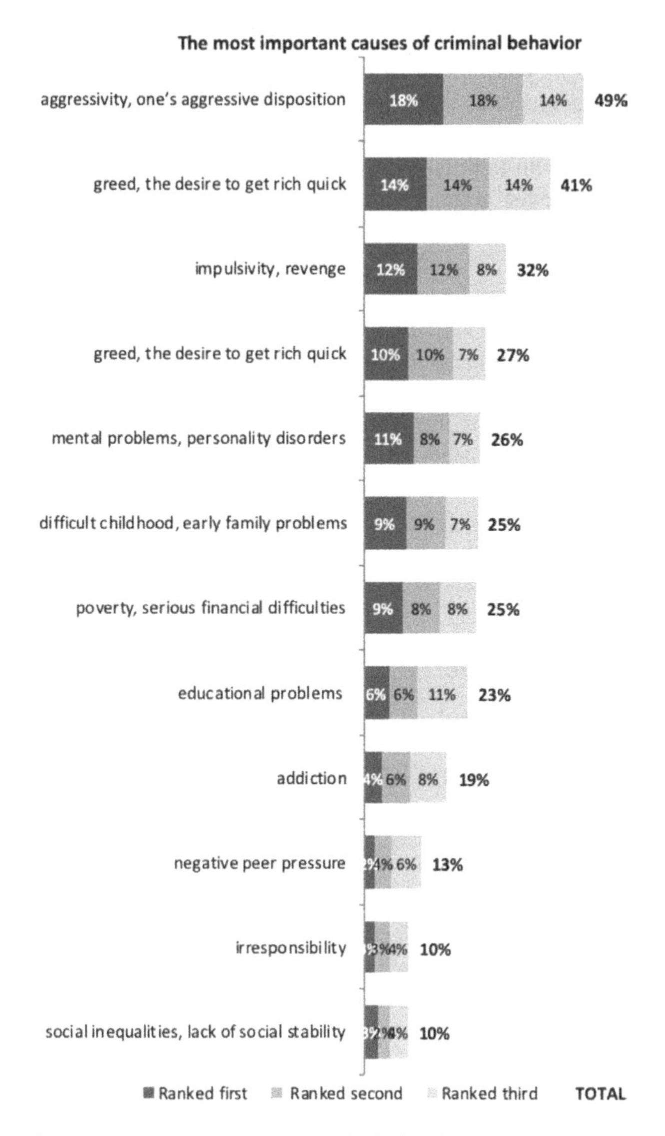

Figure 6.5 The three most important causes of criminal behavior

When we asked respondents to identify the three most important causes, quite a similar list emerged. Once again, internal factors have priority over external ones (Figure 6.5).

Multidimensional correlations

Evaluating the relevance of a given factor in criminality changes from social group to social group. The next section highlights these differences. Women attribute more significance to mental illness.[20] As a cause, poverty is more important for town dwellers than for residents in Budapest and villages.[21] Impulsivity is a more significant cause for women than for men: 90% of the female respondents believe it contributes to the process of becoming a criminal.[22] Almost all educational background groups attribute a lot of significance to impulsivity, only respondents with unfinished secondary school put slightly less emphasis on this factor, but even among them, at least 90% find it important.[23] Among respondents worst hit by financial troubles, only 77% believe that impulsivity is an essential factor.[24]

Educational problems as factors in criminal behavior appear mainly among the top choices of respondents with the worst and the best educational backgrounds.[25] Respondents with solid financial backgrounds and those who just cannot afford essential things constitute the two groups that attribute the most significance to educational problems during the process of becoming a criminal.[26] Addiction as a factor during the process of becoming a criminal is given the most emphasis in bigger towns, probably because drug addicts reside mainly in these settlements.[27] The lack of social stability is perceived as a bigger problem by town dwellers than by residents in other settlement types.[28] It is mainly women, rather than men, who think that media violence can cause criminal behavior.[29]

6.3 Crime, plaintiffs and victims

Findings from the 2018 data collection

During the 2018 data collection, 13% of the respondents reported falling victim to some sort of crime. Most respondents who answered "yes" fell victim to theft (67%). This is followed by robbery, assault and fraud. The rate of other types of crime remained below 10%.

One-third of the respondents are afraid of becoming a victim. Those who are afraid of crime (35%) fear theft, robbery and assault most. As we can see, this is the same order as the one reflecting the types of actual victimization mentioned previously. In addition to these, more than 10% of respondents mentioned fraud, harassment and computer crime.

Multidimensional correlations

The highest rate of crime victims occurs among respondents with university degrees and participants with minimal education.[30] 26% of those respondents who struggle with serious financial problems report having become victims of crime. This rate decreases with the improvement of one's finances, but it increases again among the most affluent participants (17%).[31] A significantly higher rate of women (42%) are afraid of falling victim to crime than men (28%).[32] More than half of the respondents with money troubles are afraid of being a victim of crime. This tendency decreases with the lessening of these troubles to the point where only 13% of the most affluent participants report having such fears.[33]

6.4 Attitudes toward the justice system

Findings from the 2018 data collection

A large number of respondents have formulated criticism of the justness of the law and the justice system. 82% of them believe that influential people have better chances at court, 76% think that justice and the law are two different things, and 75% claim that the personality of a judge is a key factor in legal procedures. Yet, 59% think that verdicts and sentences are acceptable. Importantly, the majority believes that lawsuits and litigation are pointless, because only barristers profit from them. 71% of the respondents allege that the justice system is not free from political influence (Figure 6.6).

Multidimensional correlations

Influential people have better chances during legal procedures in what respondents with minimal education claim, while university graduates are the most reluctant group to share this view.[34] Groups from different settlement types have different perspectives on this problem. A lower rate of Budapest dwellers and town dwellers sense the corrupting power of influence in legal matters, whereas the same rate is higher in villages and county seats.[35] It is respondents with the worst financial backgrounds who are the most likely to assume that influential people have better chances at court.[36]

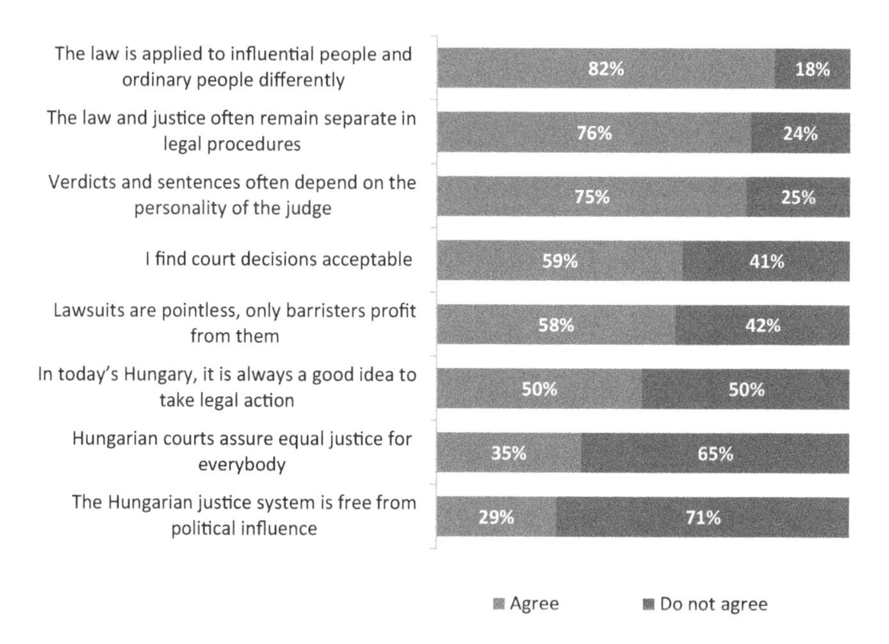

Figure 6.6 Statements about the justice system

Budapest dwellers are more likely to believe that the justice system is free from political influence than residents elsewhere.[37] The smaller a settlement is, the more likely a respondent is to assume that court decisions depend on the personality of the judge.[38] The principle of equality before the law is thought to be best applied in Budapest, where nearly 50% of respondents assume that courts assure equal justice for everybody. Elsewhere, there are no significant differences between groups and far fewer participants believe in the application of this principle.[39] Two-thirds of the respondents in the capital city find that it is always a good idea to take legal action when seeking justice. 55% of villagers agree with this, and they are followed by residents in county seats, where this rate is only 31%.[40]

Most respondents with minimum education see the role of barristers negatively. Only 43% of people with a college degree have a similar view, and among university graduates, this rate is 55%.[41] The smaller a settlement is, the more negatively its residents see the role of barristers. As many as 66% of villagers subscribe to the view that lawsuits are pointless because only barristers profit from them.[42] A similarly high rate (67%) of respondents who run out of money by the end of each month sees the role of barristers negatively. Slightly exceeding 50%, this rate is lower in other groups of financial status.[43] A high rate (73%) of Budapest dwellers finds that court decisions are acceptable. The lowest rate (47%) of acceptance was measured in regional capitals.[44] The split between justice and the law is perceived mainly in regional capitals and villages. Residents in Budapest and towns see this issue in a more favorable light.[45]

Notes

1 khi^2=0,123 p=0,002
2 khi^2=0,137 p=0,000
3 khi^2=0,075 p=0,018
4 khi^2=0,152 p=0,001
5 khi^2=0,099 p=0,021
6 khi^2=0,089 p=0,005
7 khi^2=0,102 p=0,036
8 khi^2=0,097 p=0,024
9 khi^2=0,105 p=0,012
10 khi^2=0,124 p=0,004
11 khi^2=0,089 p=0,012
12 khi^2=0,110 p=0,000
13 khi^2=0,094 p=0,010
14 khi^2=0,141 p=0,000
15 khi^2=0,171 p=0,000
16 khi^2=0,116 p=0,004
17 khi^2=0,146 p=0,000
18 khi^2=0,112 p=0,006
19 khi^2=0,105 p=0,012
20 khi^2=0,084 p=0,008
21 khi^2=0,102 p=0,016
22 khi^2=0,063 p=0,045
23 khi^2=0,098 p=0,047
24 khi^2=0,098 p=0,023

25 $khi^2=0,099$ $p=0,045$
26 $khi^2=0,092$ $p=0,037$
27 $khi^2=0,092$ $p=0,040$
28 $khi^2=0,127$ $p=0,001$
29 $khi^2=0,076$ $p=0,016$
30 $khi^2=0,165$ $p=0,000$
31 $khi^2=0,117$ $p=0,003$
32 $khi^2=0,142$ $p=0,000$
33 $khi^2=0,160$ $p=0,000$
34 $khi^2=0,108$ $p=0,020$
35 $khi^2=0,139$ $p=0,000$
36 $khi^2=0,156$ $p=0,000$
37 $khi^2=0,156$ $p=0,000$
38 $khi^2=0,106$ $p=0,010$
39 $khi^2=0,155$ $p=0,000$
40 $khi^2=0,212$ $p=0,000$
41 $khi^2=0,115$ $p=0,010$
42 $khi^2=0,153$ $p=0,000$
43 $khi^2=0,117$ $p=0,004$
44 $khi^2=0,164$ $p=0,004$
45 $khi^2=0,162$ $p=0,004$

7 Criticism of the system and worldviews

7.1 System justification and system criticism

Findings from the 2018 data collection

Our study gave us an opportunity to learn how respondents think about contemporary Hungarian society (Figure 7.1). The findings reveal that the large majority of participants find fighting against corruption necessary and nearly as many respondents would welcome a strong political leader. Interestingly, while three-quarters of the respondents think they should exercise their right to vote (this rate is hardly different from the one measured at the 2018 parliamentary elections), 72% also believe democracy in Hungary will not function properly in decades to come. In addition, a large number of participants articulate strong criticism of political parties.

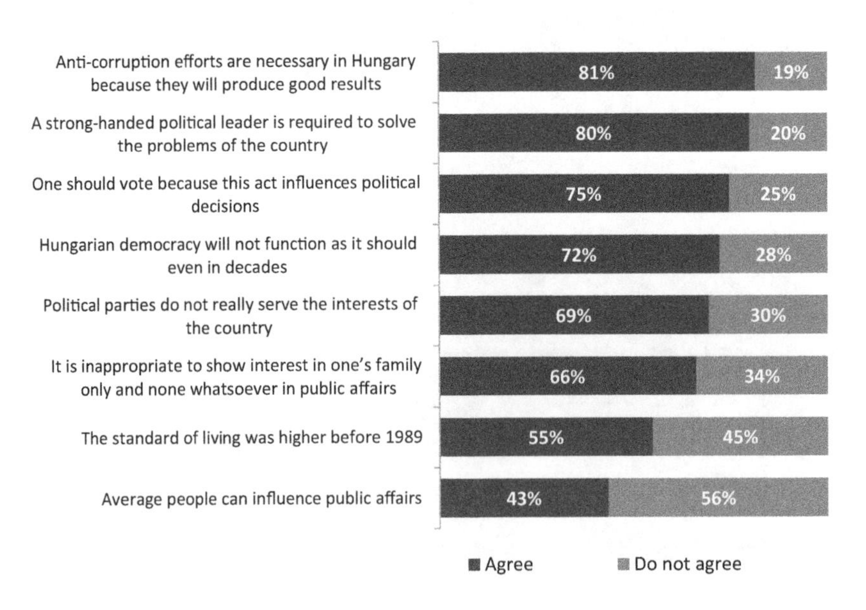

Figure 7.1 Views on Hungarian society

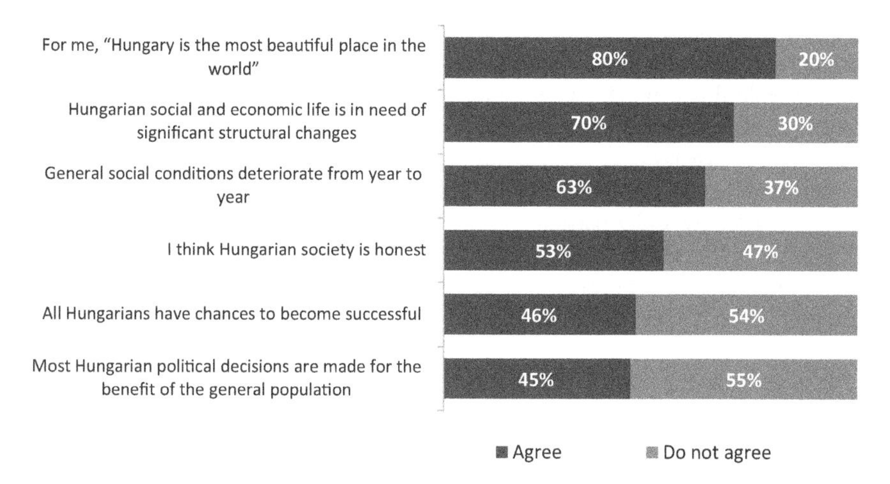

Figure 7.2 Attitudes toward Hungary

Two-thirds of the respondents believe that showing interest in one's family only and nothing whatsoever in public affairs is wrong. A small majority claim that the standard of living was higher before 1989.

A large majority of the respondents (80%) think that Hungary is the most beautiful place in the world. 70% would welcome significant structural changes in Hungarian social and economic life. This desire is also signaled by the fact that nearly two-thirds of the respondents claim that general conditions in Hungary are deteriorating. The question whether or not society as a whole is honest divides participants. A small majority find that not all people have the chance to become successful, while the majority believe that political decisions are not made for the benefit of the general population (Figure 7.2).

Based on the responses, the following image of Hungary arises. Society is active, it shows interest in public affairs and it prefers a strong political leader. At the same time, it is quite critical of the present political elite and is self-critical. It expects major improvements only after significant social and economic changes.

Multidimensional correlations

Respondents with the least schooling consider Hungarian democracy in the worst shape, and groups of more educated participants offer roughly identical opinions.[1] It is Budapest dwellers who have the most trust in the idea of a slowly improving democratic model. Elsewhere, respondents are gloomier about the future.[2] An obvious correlation can be pointed out between subjectively perceived financial background and views on democracy. Stable finances make one's outlook optimistic, while money troubles make respondents pessimistic about the future of democracy.[3] As the respondents become older, the idea of active engagement in public affairs achieves more importance. It is only in the oldest age group that less than 70% argue that it is inappropriate to show interest in one's family only and nothing whatsoever in public affairs.[4] Differences in educational background generate quite different responses in this context. Better-educated respondents will attribute more importance to active political engagement.[5] Examining subjectively perceived financial background reveals the same tendency: the more affluent respondents are, the more importance they attribute to active political engagement.[6]

Unsurprisingly, older participants are more likely to claim that the standard of living was higher before 1989, even if among respondents over sixty this tendency is less pronounced.[7] Fewer respondents in the better-educated groups will state that the standard of living was higher before 1989. Among university graduates, this rate is only 38%.[8]

It is Budapest dwellers who are the most critical of the change of regime in 1989. Around 60% of respondents in other settlement types see it as positive political transformation.[9]

While respondents with money troubles claim they had a better life before 1989, participants with a better financial background say the standard of living is now higher.[10] When exploring the link between settlement types and the individual's political competence, no clear tendencies emerge. Residents in Budapest and towns attribute greater competence to the average individual, but residents in regional capitals and villages see less room for action.[11]

Budapest dwellers think that political parties adequately serve the interests of the country. The lowest rate of agreement is in villages.[12] Affluent respondents are likely to think that political parties adequately serve the interests of the country. This likelihood decreases with worsening finances.[13] The highest rate of those who believe voting is the right thing to do can be found in the capital city, while in smaller settlements, this rate is lower and nearly identical.[14] The lowest rate of those who believe voting is the right thing to do can be found among respondents with serious money troubles, and in the other groups, this rate is above 70%.[15]

As educational background improves, the more convinced a given respondent becomes about the need for anti-corruption measures.[16] Bad finances clearly impact respondents' perspective on the need for anti-corruption measures. Participants worst hit by money troubles have no trust in these measures, not even in the long run.[17] It is respondents with the least education who count on a strong-handed political leader the most. With better education, such expectations are more limited.[18] Budapest dwellers are the most convinced about the honest nature of the Hungarian population, while respondents from regional capitals are the least convinced.[19] Interestingly, belief in the honesty of Hungarian society is the strongest among better-off respondents, it is weaker with less income, but among the poorest participants, it becomes stronger again.[20]

It is mainly the least educated group of respondents who find that Hungarian social and economic life is in definite need of significant structural changes. Fewer better-educated participants insist on this.[21] Mainly residents in regional capitals and villages call for thorough social transformation. This demand is more limited in Budapest and towns.[22] Two-thirds of Budapest dwellers find that political decisions are made for the benefit of the general population. This rate is much lower in other settlement types.[23] Chances for a better life in Hungary are perceived mainly in Budapest. There is no significant difference between other settlement types in this regard.[24] Respondents with better finances are more likely to see good chances for all Hungarians, but this perspective becomes less optimistic with worsening financial backgrounds.[25] It is mainly respondents with the least education who find that social conditions deteriorate, while participants from better-educated groups think about this issue alike.[26] A higher rate of residents in regional capitals and villages sense that social conditions deteriorate.[27] The rate of those who believe that general social conditions deteriorate from year to year grows with the worsening of the participants' subjectively perceived financial background.[28]

7.2 Belief in a just world

Findings from the 2018 data collection

Nearly two-thirds of the respondents find that the things they personally experience are basically just and, as a rule, they get what they deserve. Injustice is best seen as an exception. 58% think that injustice in all walks of life is an exception, and the same rate claims that justice will always prevail over injustice. Those who see a just world and believe they get what they deserve constitute a majority.

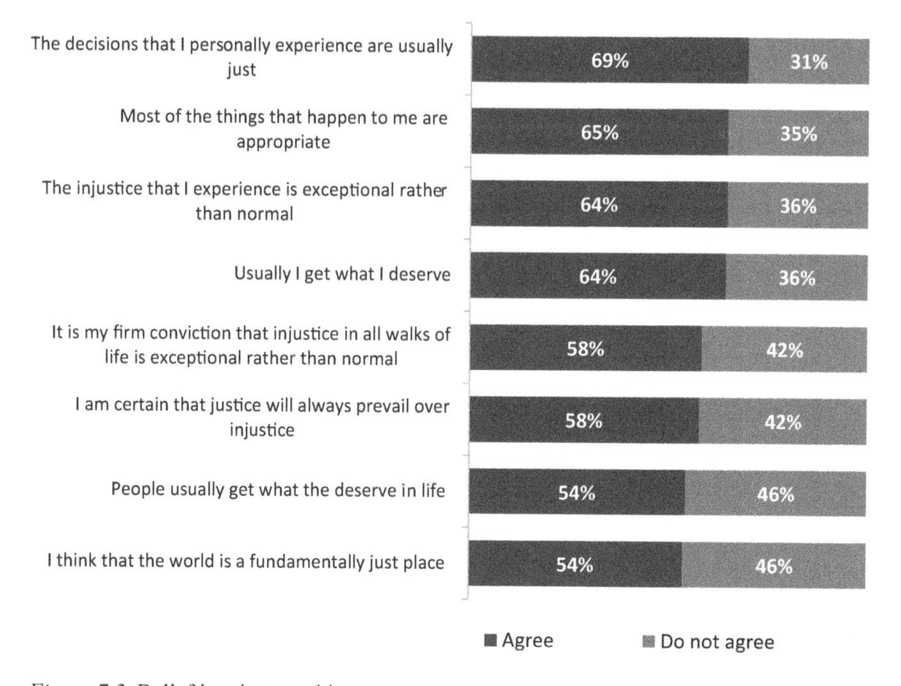

Figure 7.3 Belief in a just world

Multidimensional correlations

Those who consider the world a just place are more likely to live in Budapest and towns than elsewhere. The lowest rate of respondents to share this optimistic view can be found in regional capitals.[29] One's finances strongly influence one's belief in a just world. A higher rate of better-off respondents think the world is a just place (Figure 7.3).[30] It is again better-off participants who think that the decisions that they personally experience are usually just. With worsening finances, this rate decreases. Those respondents who have the most serious money problems and who usually find that such decisions are unjust constitute a majority.[31] It is mainly Budapest dwellers who think that they get what they deserve. Residents in regional capitals are least likely to share this view.[32]

Similarly to earlier correlations, affluent respondents find that they get what they deserve in a higher rate. As we move toward the group of the poorest, we find more and more participants who have their doubts about this.[33] A very high rate of Budapest dwellers think that injustice is exceptional. The related rates of residents in other settlement types are nearly identical.[34] Mainly residents in the capital city believe that justice will always prevail over injustice, while the most doubt about this idea is shown in regional capitals.[35] A good financial background leads to a stronger belief in the triumph of justice, while money problems produce the opposite effect.[36] 74% of Budapest dwellers think that the injustice they experience is exceptional. This rate is lower in other settlement types.[37] As shown earlier, subjectively perceived financial background has clear impact on how one experiences injustice. A higher rate of better-off respondents find injustice an exceptional event, while in the financially most vulnerable group, this view is represented only by a minority.[38] Budapest dwellers have the most positive attitude toward the key events in their lives. A somewhat lower, but still relatively high rate (around 60%) of residents in other settlement types think that most of the things that happen to them are appropriate.[39] A familiar correlation is detectable between financial background and this concept. Those who see their finances in a positive light are more likely to believe that most of the things that happen to them in life are appropriate.[40]

Notes

1 khi^2=0,100 p=0,040
2 khi^2=0,182 p=0,040
3 khi^2=0,122 p=0,002
4 khi^2=0,134 p=0,007
5 khi^2=0,134 p=0,007
6 khi^2=0,099 p=0,020
7 khi^2=0,116 p=0,007
8 khi^2=0,124 p=0,000
9 khi^2=0,162 p=0,000
10 khi^2=0,130 p=0,000
11 khi^2=0,096 p=0,005
12 khi^2=0,100 p=0,003
13 khi^2=0,093 p=0,008
14 khi^2=0,081 p=0,041

15 khi^2=0,122 p=0,000
16 khi^2=0,128 p=0,000
17 khi^2=0,126 p=0,000
18 khi^2=0,100 p=0,010
19 khi^2=0,175 p=0,000
20 khi^2=0,130 p=0,001
21 khi^2=0,100 p=0,040
22 khi^2=0,156 p=0,000
23 khi^2=0,224 p=0,000
24 khi^2=0,163 p=0,000
25 khi^2=0,162 p=0,000
26 khi^2=0,099 p=0,044
27 khi^2=0,158 p=0,000
28 khi^2=0,131 p=0,001
29 khi^2=0,157 p=0,000
30 khi^2=0,127 p=0,001
31 khi^2=0,149 p=0,001
32 khi^2=0,149 p=0,001
33 khi^2=0,165 p=0,001
34 khi^2=0,110 p=0,007
35 khi^2=0,144 p=0,007
36 khi^2=0,100 p=0,018
37 khi^2=0,105 p=0,012
38 khi^2=0,131 p=0,001
39 khi^2=0,103 p=0,014
40 khi^2=0,157 p=0,000

8 Changing views of the law and civil society between 2010 and 2018

8.1 Law, crime and the justice system

Legislation, judicial practice, death penalty and the causes of crime

Numerous changes took place after the 2010 data collection, which are considered in this chapter.

Perhaps most noticeably, two-thirds of Hungarian society supported the restoration of the death penalty in 2010, but this rate dropped quite significantly to 54% by 2018.[1] Respondents contribute more importance to increased welfare spending in relation to crime prevention in 2018 than in 2010. While earlier 35% believed this is an essential factor, by 2018, this rate is 46%.[2] The only minor change that can be observed is about attitudes toward the need for harsher sentencing. Instead of 88%, it is 82% who think that harsher sentencing deters crime. It is clear that a large majority of Hungarians still see harsh sentences as effective deterrents.[3]

Compared to earlier data collection, the average value of composite variables changed significantly. As we can tell from the difference between average values, support for prohibition and punishment decreased from 2.73 to 2.49. At the same time, the ideas of social support and legalization attracted more respondents (the rise is from 2.35 to 2.47). Thus, one can say that the average of the two composite variables became nearly identical.

Causes of crime decline

While earlier there was a consensus (84%) with regard to the idea that the lack of unemployment would lead to less crime, now this rate is only 63% (Table 8.1).[4] Similarly, the number of those who believe in the preventive function of more discipline at schools decreased from 79% to 68%.[5] In 2010, 84% of the respondents thought that tighter human communities could have a positive impact on crime prevention, but by 2018, this rate changed to 79%.[6] Perspectives on the preventive function of increased welfare spending changed significantly, too. In 2018, 49% believed in its effectiveness, while earlier it was only 40%.[7] A large majority of society still believes in the significant preventive power of harsher sentences; however, support for this idea declined from 92% to 88%.[8] A similar decline in the support

Table 8.1 Legislation-criticism – changes in average value of composite variables

MEASURE	*STATEMENTS*	*AVERAGE 1–4 point Likert scale*	
		2010	*2018*
Legislation-criticism For prohibition and punishment	Abortion should be banned The death penalty should be restored Harsher sentences would deter crime	**2.73**	**2.49**
Legislation-criticism For social support and legalization	Prison terms in themselves do not reduce crime Increased welfare spending would reduce crime significantly Mild drugs such as marihuana should be legalized	**2.35**	**2.47**

Table 8.2 Crime prevention – changes in average value of composite variables

MEASURE	*STATEMENTS*	*AVERAGE 1–4 point Likert scale*	
		2010	*2018*
Crime prevention through improved circumstances	Lack of unemployment Tighter human communities Increased welfare spending	**2.88**	**2.74**
Crime prevention through determent and harsher measures	More discipline at schools Harsher sentencing Stricter criminal laws	**3.39**	**3.18**

for harsher sentencing can be observed in the support for harsher criminal laws. The drop is from 91% to 87%.[9] The average value of both composite variables decreased significantly, which means that Hungarian society has less belief in crime prevention. More people believe that neither better social circumstances nor harsher sentencing (or any other deterrents) lead to less crime (Table 8.2).

Becoming a criminal

The changes that occurred after the 2010 data collection also demonstrate that society tends to attach more significance to the subjective factors behind criminal behavior (Table 8.3). In this context, poverty as an explanation is acceptable for fewer people (76%) than it was before (80%).[10] The role of impulsivity – a subjective factor – is given more emphasis (from 86% to 92%).[11] Even if only minimally, the emphasis given to aggressivity grew, too (from 94% to 96%).[12]

Table 8.3 Causes of criminal behavior – changes in average value of composite variables

MEASURE	*STATEMENT*	*AVERAGE 1–4 point Likert scale*	
		2010	*2018*
Causes of criminal behavior – Psychological	Mental problems, personality disorders Impulsivity, revenge Aggressivity, one's aggressive disposition Addiction	**3.28**	**3.36**
Causes of criminal behavior – Social	Difficult childhood, early family problems Poverty, serious financial difficulties Educational problems Social inequalities, lack of social stability	**3.13**	**3.10**
Causes of criminal behavior – External control	Greed, the desire to get rich quick Irresponsibility Negative peer pressure Media violence	**3.22**	**3.18**

Correspondingly, a higher number of respondents stressed the role of addiction, another psychological problem (82% earlier, now 86%).[13] Compared to 2010, the lack of social stability is given much less significance. The rate of those who find it a key explanation declined from 78% to 70%.[14] A similar drop is detectable in significance attributed to media violence. While earlier 81% found it an essential cause behind criminal behavior, by 2018 it is 70%.[15]

Studying changes in composite variables reveals that the two data collections differ mainly in the evaluation of the function of psychological factors. Respondents continue to think about the role of social factors and external control as before. Psychological factors were deemed important earlier, too, and now their importance grew. Thus, the earlier 3.28 average value rose to 3.36. The average value of the other two composite variables did not change significantly, so the impact of external control has the second highest value (3.18), followed by social factors (3.1).

The same tendency to put more emphasis on internal factors and less on external ones can be observed in the list of the most important causes behind criminality. The only exception is difficult childhood, which is an external factor with a ranking higher than before.

Crime, plaintiffs and victims

Compared to 2010, a lower rate of respondents reported falling victim to crime. While the earlier rate was 19%, this time it is 13%. This shift may be attributed to a decrease in the perception of crime, rather than the actual number of victims, because the social structure did not change significantly during this period.[16] As seen

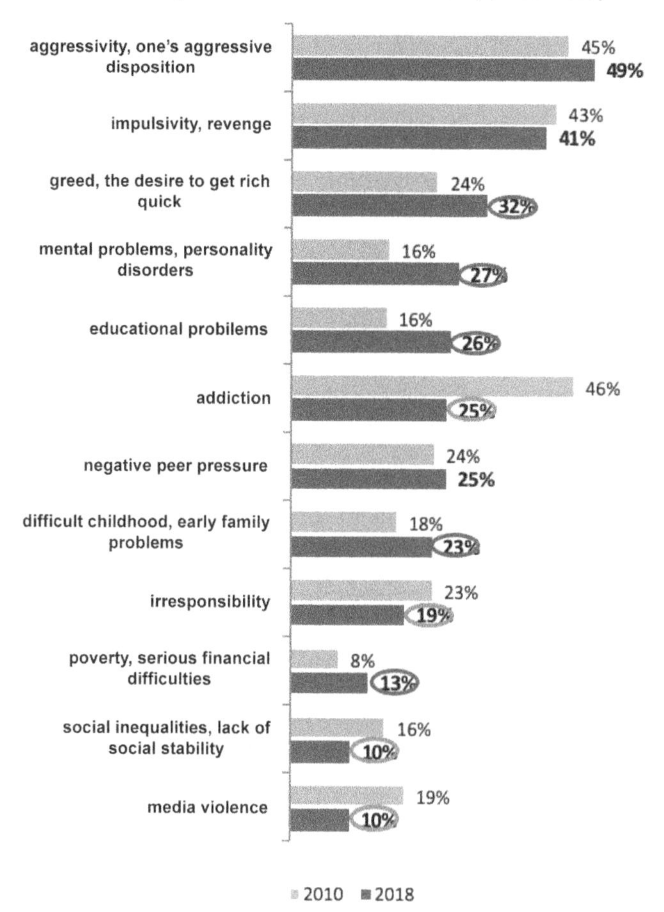

Figure 8.1 Most important causes behind criminality: 2010–2018

Figure 8.1, theft continues to be the crime mentioned by the highest rate of respondents. The earlier hypothesis that real change took place in the perception of crime and not so much in actual exposure to crime can be upheld here, too. Respondents are significantly less afraid of becoming a victim; therefore, the 2010 rate of 58% dropped nearly to its half by 35%.[17] There is significantly less mention of theft, robbery and assault, and there is slightly more mention of fraud and computer crime.

Attitudes toward the justice system

Less political influence has been attributed to the justice system since 2010 (Table 8.4). In that year, 79% of the respondents assumed that the justice system has no political

Table 8.4 Acceptance of the justice system – changes in average value of composite variables

MEASURE	*STATEMENT*	*AVERAGE* 1–4 *point Likert scale*	
		2010	*2018*
Acceptance of the justice system	The law is applied to influential people and ordinary people differently The Hungarian justice system is free from political influence Verdicts and sentences often depend on the personality of the judge Hungarian courts assure equal justice for everybody In today's Hungary, it is always a good idea to take legal action Lawsuits are pointless, only barristers profit from them I find court decisions acceptable The law and justice often remain separate in legal procedures	**2.04**	**2.18**

independence; by now, this rate is down to 71%.[18] According to respondents, the principle of equal justice for everybody has asserted itself more markedly over this period. The rate of those who believe this concept actually prevails rose from 28% to 35%.[19] As in the previous tendency, there is a higher number of people who believe it is a good idea to take legal action. While in 2018, 36% thought so, now this rate is 50%.[20] The role of barristers in legal procedures has been seen in an increasingly favorable light. In 2010, 70% of the respondents believed it was not worth starting litigation or a lawsuit, but in 2018, this rate is 58%.[21] While earlier court decisions divided Hungarian society to a great extent, in 2018, the majority of respondents (59%) agree with them.[22]

Respondents see a closer link between the law and the concept of justice in 2018 than earlier, even if the large majority of them claim these two still remain separate.[23] Studying changes in composite variables reveals that respondents have a more positive attitude toward the justice system, with the earlier 2.04 average value rising to 2.18 by 2018.

8.2 Criticism of the system and worldviews

System justification and system criticism

The previous statements acquire special meanings in relation to the changes that took place after 2010. Respondents see the state of democracy more positively because the rate of those who think that Hungarian democracy will not function adequately in the foreseeable future dropped from 79% to 72%.[24] A more marked change occurred in the comparison of standards of living before and after 1989. While earlier 76% of the respondents assumed that the standard of living was higher before the change of regime, by 2018, it was 55%.[25]

All in all, more people sense that they can influence public affairs. Only every third respondent had this feeling in 2010, but by 2018, this rate is 43%.[26] Political parties are also seen in a less hostile light. The earlier rate of critics decreased from 82% to 69%.[27] Anti-corruption efforts continue to enjoy major social support, but a slight decline is detectable from 88% in 2010 to 81% in 2018.[28] The demand for a strong political leader decreased slightly, but 80% of the respondents still claim that only such a person can solve the problems of the country.[29] Belief in the honest, law-abiding character of Hungarian society has grown stronger. A one-third minority is now a majority.[30] The social–economic structure of Hungarian society is also seen in a more positive light. In 2010, 92% of the respondents claimed that it needed a major overhaul, but by 2018, this rate was only 70%.[31] Respondents view political decisions more positively. Earlier only 19% of them believed that they are made for the benefit of the general population, by 2018, this rate is 45%.[32] There is more positivity associated with individual chances and ambitions. In 2010, every fourth participant thought that all Hungarians have the chance to become successful, this rate is 46% in 2018.[33] Even if two-thirds of the respondents still find that general social conditions deteriorate from year to year, this rate has significant improvement in comparison to the earlier 86%.[34] The change in composite variables shows an increasingly accepting attitude toward the present system (Table 8.5). The average value of system criticism decreased from 2.71 to 2.57, while the average

Table 8.5 System criticism – changes in average value of composite variables

MEASURE	*STATEMENT*	*AVERAGE 1–4 point Likert scale*	
		2010	*2018*
System criticism	Hungarian democracy will not function as it should even in decades to come It is inappropriate to show interest in one's family only and none whatsoever in public affairs The standard of living was higher before 1989 Average people can influence public affairs Political parties do not really serve the interests of the country One should vote because this act influences political decisions Anti-corruption efforts are necessary in Hungary because they will produce good results A strong-handed political leader is required to solve the problems of the country	**2.71**	**2.57**

Table 8.6 System justification – changes in average value of composite variables

MEASURE	*STATEMENT*	*AVERAGE 1–4 point Likert scale*	
		2010	*2018*
System justification	I think Hungarian society is honest Hungarian social and economic life is in need of significant structural changes For me, "Hungary is the most beautiful place in the world" Most Hungarian political decisions are made for the benefit of the general population All Hungarians have chances to become successful General social conditions deteriorate from year to year	**2.05**	**2.44**

value of system justification follows an inverse pattern through its increase from 2.05 to 2.44 (Table 8.6).

Belief in a just world

The rate of those who believe our world is a just place has grown from 40% to 54% since 2010.[35] The number of those who believe that people usually get what they deserve in life also grew. Compared to the earlier 43%, it is 54% of respondents in 2018.[36] In 2010, 57% of respondents assumed that the decisions that they personally experienced were usually just. By 2018, this rate rose to 69%.[37]

While Hungarian society in 2010 was quite divided on the issue whether or not people got what they deserved, this changed drastically by 2018 and nearly two-thirds of the respondents claimed the distribution of wealth happened on the basis of merit.[38] There is a slight rise (to 58%) in the rate of those who see injustice as an exceptional event in their lives.[39] Significantly, the rate of those who believe that justice will always prevail over injustice rose from 39% to 58%.[40] Respondents who thought the injustice that they experienced was exceptional rather than normal formed a majority already in 2010. This rate reached 64% by 2018.[41] 65% of respondents in 2018 felt that most of the things that happened to them were appropriate, which is a 10% rise from the 55% measured in 2010.[42] Belief in a just world is also more common than earlier. The average value of both measures (one exploring a personal dimension, another a general) grew. The value of the general measure rose from 2.35 to 2.58, while the earlier high value (2.54) of the personal dimension continued to rise to reach 2.71 in 2018 (Table 8.7).

Table 8.7 Belief in a just world – changes in average value of composite variables

MEASURE	*STATEMENT*	*AVERAGE 1–4 point Likert scale*	
		2010	*2018*
Belief in a just world – General	I think that the world is a fundamentally just place People usually get what they deserve in life It is my firm conviction that injustice in all walks of life (e.g. workplace, family or politics) is exceptional rather than normal I am certain that justice will always prevail over injustice	**2.35**	**2.58**
Belief in a just world – Personal	The important decisions that I personally experience are usually just Usually I get what I deserve The injustice that I experience in life is exceptional rather than normal Most of the things that happen to me in life are appropriate	**2.53**	**2.71**

Notes

1 khi^2=0,131 p=0,000
2 khi^2=0,122 p=0,000
3 khi^2=0,084 p=0,000
4 khi^2=0,223 p=0,000
5 khi^2=0,124 p=0,000
6 khi^2=0,061 p=0,006
7 khi^2=0,092 p=0,000
8 khi^2=0,058 p=0,010
9 khi^2=0,059 p=0,008
10 khi^2=0,048 p=0,031
11 khi^2=0,100 p=0,000
12 khi^2=0,067 p=0,003
13 khi^2=0,048 p=0,033
14 khi^2=0,093 p=0,000
15 khi^2=0,130 p=0,000
16 khi^2=0,080 p=0,000
17 khi^2=0,222 p=0,000
18 khi^2=0,096 p=0,000
19 khi^2=0,075 p=0,001
20 khi^2=0,136 p=0,000
21 khi^2=0,125 p=0,000
22 khi^2–0,094 p–0,000
23 khi^2=0,054 p=0,016
24 khi^2=0,082 p=0,000

25 $khi^2=0,225$ $p=0,000$
26 $khi^2=0,127$ $p=0,004$
27 $khi^2=0,169$ $p=0,000$
28 $khi^2=0,057$ $p=0,039$
29 $khi^2=0,089$ $p=0,000$
30 $khi^2=0,231$ $p=0,000$
31 $khi^2=0,281$ $p=0,000$
32 $khi^2=0,275$ $p=0,000$
33 $khi^2=0,231$ $p=0,000$
34 $khi^2=0,266$ $p=0,000$
35 $khi^2=0,138$ $p=0,000$
36 $khi^2=0,111$ $p=0,000$
37 $khi^2=0,129$ $p=0,000$
38 $khi^2=0,132$ $p=0,000$
39 $khi^2=0,050$ $p=0,024$
40 $khi^2=0,188$ $p=0,024$
41 $khi^2=0,071$ $p=0,002$
42 $khi^2=0,095$ $p=0,000$

9 Correlations and conclusions

In this chapter, we summarize the main findings of our study and compare them to the results of the 2010 study to identify key changes and correlations.

9.1 Getting informed

Nearly two-thirds of society show interest, on some level, in recent political events and topical social issues. In the category of printed newspapers, the following three sensational papers attract the largest number of readers: *Blikk*, *Story* and *Bors*. Specifically political papers are read by less than 5% of respondents. The most widely read, *Blikk*, is also the most credible newspaper. It is followed by the political weekly *HVG* in the credibility ranking. *Blikk* is also seen as the least credible source of information. It indicates that the position of *Blikk* is unquestionable on the printed press market. Studying credibility measures, we can also see that political newspapers are seen in a much more positive light and that *HVG*, *Népszava*, *Szabad Föld* and *Magyar Hírlap* are the leading publications in this regard.

By reference to news programs, the two big commercial channels – RTL and TV2 – have the highest ratings. The leading show is provided by RTL, followed by TV2 Tények. These two are then followed by the news programs of the national television channels. The M1 news program is seen as the most credible show, and the RTL news program as the least credible one. As ranked by credibility measures, M1, Hír TV and RTL broadcast the most reliable news programs. Most respondents visit Index.hu and Origo.hu. These two websites are seen as the most credible ones, even if they, simultaneuously, rank quite high among the least credible websites. 888.hu is the leading website in this latter, negative context. As ranked by credibility measures, HVG.hu, Origo, Index and 24.hu stand out.

Today, the internet is one of the most important sources of information. For this reason, we found it important to examine how many respondents go online and how much time they spend there. One-quarter of society uses the internet for business purposes on weekdays, averaging 3.2 hours per day. Nearly every other respondent uses the internet for non-business purposes, such as social media, averaging 2 hours per day. Only 10% of the participants go online for business purposes on weekends, averaging about 2.5 hours per day. Every other person uses the internet for non-business purposes on weekends, averaging 2.6 hours per day.

9.2 Party preferences

The Fidesz-KDNP party alliance continues to be the most popular. It is followed by Jobbik, MSZP and DK. Oddly, Fidesz-KDNP is also the party rejected by the highest rate of respondents. On this negative scale, they are followed by the same parties as the ones listed earlier. This demonstrates vividly how deeply party preferences divide Hungarian society.

9.3 Individual and society – distribution and expectations

Responses indicate that the majority of Hungarians would support the idea of a performance-based distribution of resources in the form of progressive taxation. However, this is a more complex situation because the idea of equal distribution of wealth also has strong support. In addition, a large number of respondents feel that most Hungarians face increasing difficulties and, in their struggles, they can count neither on others nor on public administration, even if a large majority of participants assert that it is easy to find new friends. As part of this worldview, almost 40% of respondents believe that it is irresponsible to have children under the current circumstances.

Flat rate taxation has the biggest support – perhaps surprisingly – among Budapest dwellers, while the idea of progressive taxation is the most popular with residents in regional capitals. Respondents in small settlements, with little education or with serious money troubles, are the most likely to feel they cannot influence social processes. Those who are in the most disadvantaged groups in terms of income, education or settlement type are also quite gloomy about individual chances in general. The reason for this has to do with their overall situation and their previous negative experiences. In other words, respondents from these groups are defined by an unfavorable background. This, in turn, prevents them from improving their situations, and as a consequence, the social distance between them and others continues to grow. As their responses demonstrate, nearly everyone in these groups feels that ordinary people are worse off than before and living like there is no tomorrow is the only option.

9.4 Individual and society – effects of globalization

A high rate of respondents considered each of the problems listed on the questionnaire grave. Environmental pollution, global warming, terrorism, migration and deepening social inequalities are seen as particularly pressing problems. Migration, which has been a central topic in recent public discourse, provokes strong opinions in contemporary Hungarian society. The majority of Hungarians approve of defending their present way of life, along with the restriction of foreigners' rights and fears about the crimes foreigners may commit. Correspondingly, a majority of respondents reject the positive effects of globalization. It is mainly city-dwelling participants with poor finances who perceive more serious social problems. Because certain problems exert only long-term effects, such as environmental pollution, their gravity is more likely to be recognized by better-educated respondents. Fearing other cultures is characteristic of those who live in Budapest, villagers, respondents with minimal education and participants with serious money troubles, whereas openness to other cultures is associated with youth, better education and residence in regional capitals.

9.5 Individual and society – self-characterization

When it comes to self-characterization, the Hungarian population is quite divided: financial situation and educational background are key factors. As we saw earlier, being deprived has a powerful impact on one's self-image, self-esteem, general outlook on life and even one's ability to act in certain situations. Low self-esteem can prevent people from achieving success because people who cannot handle complex situations and prefer to avoid them will not be able to rise above their social limitations and this kind of "acquired inertia" contributes to the preservation of the existing social hierarchy. The questionnaires indicate clearly that approximately every fifth Hungarian is deprived and, for this reason, these respondents have low self-esteem and are permanently frustrated.

9.6 Law, crime and the justice system

Legislation and judicial practice

An overwhelming majority of Hungarians believe that harsher court sentences deter crime; however, they do not think that prison terms in themselves could reduce crime. When it comes to the positive effects of increased welfare spending, Hungarian society is very divided. One-third of the respondents are in favor of legalizing mild drugs. Attitudes toward social problems show a mixed picture, but as a rule, one can claim that those in favor of social support and liberalization are young, live in regional capitals and have better education. Conversely, those who are in favor of a tougher stance tend to be males with limited finances and low-level education. Most Hungarians believe in the crime prevention effects of the threat of punishment. Nearly 90% of the respondents believe that a tough penal code and harsh court sentences are essential for reducing crime. Two-thirds of them call for stricter school education and full employment to fight crime, while nearly 80% of them think close-knit communities are helpful in this respect. At the same time, only 49% believe in the beneficial effects of increased welfare spending.

The death penalty

The restoration of the death penalty is another key issue. At present, a 54% majority of Hungarians believe it was right to abolish it. When reviewing the related attitudes, one finds that 30% of the respondents believe restoring the death penalty would be just and 24% think that it would provide an effective deterrent. For 18%, this kind of punishment is unacceptable because it is not a deterrent, whereas for 22% capital punishment is objectionable because the state does not have the right to take anybody's life.

The reasons behind less crime

Those who believe that the most effective way to fight crime is by increasing welfare spending live mostly in towns and the capital city. They tend to belong to groups with very good or very bad financial backgrounds. Interestingly, stricter measures are also the most popular deterrents with these respondents, which might mean that participants from these groups believe crime must be dealt with on the level of measures, while most respondents from other groups favor alternative solutions. This does not mean, however, that the latter groups do not consider such measures legitimate; rather, it merely means that for them, they are less adequate.

The reasons behind criminality

What can make one become a criminal? What factors define this process? Hungarians believe that inner, subjective factors play the primary role. Among the leading causes, they list aggressivity, a violent disposition, impulsivity, greed and mental disorders. External factors appear only at the end of the list and include media violence, a lack of social stability and poverty. Settlement types and gender have the most significant impact on how people perceive the causes of crime. Both Budapesters and villagers approach this problem by attributing less importance to social factors, while women tend to be more aware of psychological factors of criminality than men.

Victims of crime

13% of the respondents fell victim to crime, mainly theft. One-third of all participants are afraid of becoming a victim, especially to theft, which is followed by robbery.

Acceptance of the justice system

When reviewing statements about the justice system, one can see that a significant number of them formulate criticism. These responses are mainly complaints about injustice and favoritism. Nevertheless, 50% believe it is a good idea to take legal action, while 59% of them claim that court sentences are acceptable. Critical attitudes concerning the justice system are detectable especially in regional capitals and villages, although limited educational opportunities and poverty also play a role.

9.7 System criticism and worldview

System criticism

A majority of Hungarians believe that anti-corruption efforts are important, and they prefer to delegate this task to a strong leader. Voting is important, too, even if the same respondents are of the opinion that democracy will not function properly even in decades to come. Indeed, significant frustration can be felt about political parties. Yet, the very same respondents consider Hungary the most beautiful place in the world and this remains the case even if the majority perceive grave problems in the structure of society and think that the social conditions worsen from year to year. In other words, they remain to some degree nationalistic, without necessarily believing in the capabilities of the state to function, especially with regard to justice and civil society. Indeed, it is respondents living in villages and regional capitals, who have little education and limited finances, that have the least favorable perspective on democracy and Hungarian society; it seems that in these groups, the difficulties they experience individually are projected onto society, while also seeing society as a cause of their difficulties.

Worldview

A majority of participants think they live in a just world where everybody gets what he or she deserves. However, the remaining 30–40% believe that the world is unjust and that they do not deserve what happens to them.

As was the case with system criticism, belief in a just world is the weakest with respondents who have bad financial backgrounds, little education and residence either in regional capitals or villages.

9.8 Changes

Changes in law, crime and the justice system

Legislation and law enforcement

Significantly, in 2018, a 54% drop can be observed in support for the reintroduction of the death penalty as compared with the 2010 data collection, which indicated that two-thirds of the respondents would support the reintroduction of capital punishment. Yet, in 2018, 82% still have the impression that stricter sentencing would lead to a lower crime rate, while nearly half of society (47%) believe that increased welfare spending might reduce crime. Looking at composite variables, prohibitions and the threat of punishment have less support than in 2010, and at the same time, steps taken in the direction of support and legalization attract more societal approval.

Reasons behind less crime

Between 2010 and 2018, expectations regarding the preventive effects of full employment on crime have been lowered, although two-thirds of society still believe that this might lead to less crime. The reason behind this change may be that although the unemployment rate has improved since 2010, the crime rate remained the same. Similarly, one can see a weakening in the link between the idea of less crime and stricter school education, harsher court sentences, a stricter penal code and tighter communities. Only expectations concerning the preventive effects of increased welfare spending are minimally higher. Therefore, it is not surprising that composite variables show a shift in this direction. Between 2010 and 2018, it has become clear that people no longer believe social improvement – even if it were to happen – would equate to a lower rate of crime, nor do the majority of people now believe that prohibition and harsh deterrence would lead to a lower crime rate. Indeed, the decline of trust in the effectiveness of tough measures is bigger than in the case of the previous group. All in all, this data suggests fewer and fewer Hungarians believe that the current crime rate can be reduced.

Causes behind criminality

The rate of those who emphasize psychological factors in the process of becoming a criminal is rising. While psychology was the most important explanation for participants in 2010, it has become even more important because the general consensus on the other two dimensions has not changed. Therefore, external control is the second and social situations are the third most important causes of crime. Compared to the earlier data collection, fewer respondents reported falling victim to crime and fearing becoming a victim.

Attitudes toward the justice system

Trust in the justice system continues to be low. The majority believe that influential people have better chances at court; that the law and justice are two different things; that the personality of a judge is a key factor in legal procedures; and that taking legal action is pointless. A somewhat higher rate of participants believe the justice system is free from political influence, but this is still only 29%. However, in 2018, a considerably higher number of respondents (about 50%) believe lawsuits and litigation can lead to favorable results. As the significant increase in composite variables shows, there has been some positive change in attitudes in comparison with the 2010 data collection. On the whole, however, the perception the Hungarian justice system continues to be negative.

System criticism and worldview

System criticism

The rate of those who think that Hungarian democracy will not function adequately in the foreseeable future dropped from 79% to 72%. A comparably significant change took place among those who think that the standard of living was higher before 1989. While they represented 76% of all respondents in 2010, in 2018, the same rate is 55%. A sense of participation also increased. In 2010, only every third respondent believed he or she could influence public affairs, by 2018, this rate is

43%. A more positive attitude toward political parties is detectable, too, even if only 39% of respondents claim to be satisfied with them. Anti-corruption efforts enjoy major support, although there has been a slight decrease in the number of supporters (nevertheless, 81% are still in favor). 80% of the respondents (4% less than 2010) believe that only a strong leader can solve the country's problems. In the meantime, the participants' belief in the honesty of society became stronger, rising from 30% to 54%.

The perspective on the structure of Hungarian society and economy has also undergone a positive change. While 92% of the respondents thought that this structure calls for a radical transformation in 2010, only 70% shared this view in 2018. The general attitude toward political decisions also improved. The rate of those who find that political decisions are made for the benefit of the general population rose from 19% to 45%. Parallel to this, nearly the same degree of increase can be observed among those who believe all Hungarians have a chance to become successful. At the same time, two-thirds of the respondents claim that general conditions in Hungary are deteriorating. But even here, there is a slight improvement compared with 2010. In sum, the overall picture is clearly more positive than during the 2010 data collection. This is illustrated by changes in the related variable composites. While the average value of system criticism decreased, the same measure of system justification rose significantly in comparison to the situation eight years ago.

Worldview

The percentage of those who think they live in a just world grew from 40% to 54%. The number of those who believe they get what they deserve in life also increased. Nearly 70% feel that the decisions they experience personally are just. In the divided Hungarian society of 2018, a clear majority feel that they get what they deserve. Similarly, a majority of respondents believe in the final triumph of justice, even though they constituted a minority earlier. An overwhelming majority of Hungarians perceive injustice as exceptional, which again shows a slight improvement, even if this was basically the case already in 2010. All the attributes of a just world that we examined have increased over the past eight years. The average values of the composite variables increased significantly both in the general and in the personal dimensions. This is in harmony with the kind of changes we experienced about system criticism and system justification.

Correlations between law, crime, the justice system and the idea of a just world and changes in these correlations

The correlation between the individual composite variables highlights similarities between attitudes in the examined fields and reveals how a given attitude connects with other attitudes, while also allowing the examination of these attitudes on a temporal scale. The coefficient value of the Pearson correlation chart details all these in Table No. 8. A positive value shows correlation in an identical direction,

Table 9.1 Changes between 2010 and 2018

	FINDINGS IN 2018 VERSUS 2010	*CHANGE*
Legislation and law enforcement	Less support for prohibition and threat of punishment More are in favor of support and legalization	↓ ↑
Death penalty	54% are in favor as opposed to the earlier two-thirds	↓
Reasons behind less crime	Less trust in the positive, crime preventing effects of improved circumstances Less trust in deterrence and harsher punishment	↓ ↓
Causes behind criminality	More emphasis on the role of psychological factors No change in the role of external controls No change in the role of social causes	↑ – –
Attitudes toward the justice system	The overall picture is still very negative, but it is somewhat more positive than in 2010	↑
System criticism	The current view continues to be negative, but with some positive changes in comparison to the 2010 data collection	↑
Worldview	A clearly positive worldview replaced the earlier, negative view	↑

whereas a negative value shows correlation in the opposite direction (Table 9.1). The closer their absolute value is to 1, the stronger is the correlation. System criticism is in negative correlation with the acceptance of the justice system, so those who are critical of the system are less accepting of the justice system. This correlation has become stronger since 2010, when a similar correlation can be observed between system criticism and both dimensions of belief in a just world. Critics of the system are less likely to believe in a just world, but the strength of this correlation did not change. However, the negative correlation with system justification became stronger in the sense that critics of the system articulate their criticism more powerfully than before.

These values confirm a point that the analysis of party preferences data have already revealed. Support for the political system is strong in Hungary, but those with system critical attitudes have increasingly strong convictions. Hungarian society is becoming increasingly polarized and perspectives on the system swing between extreme values. As in 2010, a positive correlation appears between the punishing or prohibitive dimension of legislation and those who want to reduce crime by improving social circumstances. This correlation did not change between 2010 and 2018. A similar correlation can be observed between the supportive, legalizing attitude of legislation and the harsh, deterrent dimension of crime prevention. As before, the strength of this correlation remained the same, although one would expect the harsher aspect of crime prevention to be associated with the prohibitive character of legislation. But even this correlation becomes explicable because if harsher legislation can prevent crime, then legislation can move in a supportive direction.

The acceptance of the justice system is positively correlated with both the social and the personal dimensions of the belief in a just world, even if the strength of the social dimension declined, and as a result, both show equal strength in 2018. In addition, there is a strong, positive correlation between system justification and the acceptance of the justice system. These correlations show unambiguously that those who accept the political system accept the related justice system and, as a result, they see a just world around them. The psychological cause behind becoming a criminal is positively and strongly correlated with the other two dimensions. In other words, whoever recognizes the role of psychological factors will also recognize the role of social and external controls. Beyond this, another correlation emerges, one that did not appear in the 2010 data collection. This measures the harsher dimension of crime prevention. According to this correlation, those who link crime to psychological factors will attempt to prevent it through tightening laws.

The assessment of social causes is related to the concept of social control, and this relation has strengthened since the earlier data collection. In addition, this dimension is correlated with the concept that aims to prevent crime through improved social circumstances, which is a logical correlation in that it aspires to handle social influences through better circumstances. Not yet existing in 2010, a new correlation appears by reference to the belief in the significance of external control and it shows itself in relation to improved circumstances. Moreover, this dimension is correlated with the punitive dimension of crime prevention, which is nothing new. These correlations indicate that Hungarian society has begun to embrace an attitude, which calls for external controls, accepts these controls and sees them as possible solutions to all social ills, a correlation that existed with much the same strength and direction in 2010. The general dimension of the belief in a just world is correlated with the personal dimension and system justification. In other words, whoever believes in a just world in general will also hold that the things that happen to him or her are appropriate. Such a respondent will justify the system, a correlation that has not changed since 2010. The belief in a just world is positively correlated with system justification. This correlation has become stronger since 2010.

In conclusion, most Hungarians perceive the changes that have taken place since 2010 positively. They still expect centralized authorities to solve social problems through legislation, rather than assuming that an individual might bring about improvements in their own living conditions and/or opportunities. Since the current regime lives up to this ideal, a majority is satisfied with it, believing they live in a more just world than before. At the same time, existing attitudes critical of the system have become much stronger, although they have not greatly increased in percentile terms. In other words, opinions are very polarized and political division is growing.

Indeed, the gap between two radically different perceptions of the institutions of civil society and the rule of law in Hungary – one classically liberal in nature and one tending toward the authoritarian – became significantly more pronounced between 2010 and 2018. Intriguingly, during this very period, the Hungarian government increasingly aligned itself with the so-called "illiberal democracies" of the former Eastern Bloc, a political and cultural alignment that seemingly has already had an effect on how individuals perceive themselves and their society. A strength of this book's method is that it enables an understanding of the shifts in legal and civic culture from the perspective of the people, which we described as a worm's-eye view in the Introduction, rather than imposing abstract concepts on the shifting complexities of social reality. What remains necessary, however, is a much broader survey of post-socialist nations. Not only would such a survey provide insights into their population's perceptions of civil society and the rule of law after socialism (and, frequently, in an increasingly illiberal political landscape), but it would also make it possible to isolate local particularities in each population's perceptions of the seismic social shifts that have taken place (Table 9.2).

Table 9.2 Correlational patterns between variables

PEARSON CORRELATIONS	SYSTEM CRITICISM		LEGISLATION-CRITICISM. IN FAVOR OF PROHIBITION AND PUNISHMENT		LEGISLATION-CRITICISM. IN FAVOR OF SUPPORT AND LEGALIZATION		ACCEPTANCE OF THE JUSTICE SYSTEM		CAUSES OF BECOMING A CRIMINAL. PSYCHOLOGICAL ONES		CAUSES OF BECOMING A CRIMINAL. SOCIAL ONES		CAUSES OF BECOMING A CRIMINAL. EXTERNAL CONTROL		CRIME PREVENTION. IMPROVED CIRCUMSTANCES		CRIME PREVENTION. TIGHTENING AND DETERRENCE		BELIEF IN A JUST WORLD. GENERAL		BELIEF IN A JUST WORLD. PERSONAL		SYSTEM JUSTIFICATION	
	2010	2018	2010	2018	2010	2018	2010	2018	2010	2018	2010	2018	2010	2018	2010	2018	2010	2018	2010	2018	2010	2018	2010	2018
System criticism	1	1	−0.017	0.045	0.141	0.040	−0.331	−0.499	0.056	0.009	0.024	0.135	0.014	0.131	−0.095	−0.079	0.052	−0.017	−0.293	−0.323	−0.232	−0.287	−0.336	−0.528
Legislation-criticism. In favor of prohibition and punishment	−0.017	0.045	1	1	0.117	0.127	−0.046	−0.085	−0.024	0.021	0.037	0.121	0.057	0.026	0.261	0.272	0.017	−0.078	0.020	−0.045	−0.018	−0.118	−0.019	−0.119
Legislation-criticism. In favor of support and legalization	0.141	0.040	0.117	0.127	1	1	−0.141	0.029	0.013	0.113	0.031	−0.035	0.097	−0.022	0.020	0.008	0.326	0.292	−0.092	0.117	−0.051	0.060	−0.128	0.119
Acceptance of the justice system	−0.331	−0.499	−0.046	−0.085	−0.141	0.029	1	1	−0.016	−0.043	−0.008	−0.070	−0.119	−0.138	−0.009	0.107	−0.114	0.061	0.453	0.384	0.387	0.337	0.469	0.576
Causes of becoming a criminal. Psychological ones	0.055	0.009	−0.024	0.021	0.013	0.113	−0.016	−0.043	1	1	0.424	0.623	0.472	0.611	0.113	0.170	0.190	0.353	0.168	0.138	0.094	0.112	−0.032	0.049

(Continued)

Table 9.2 (Continued)

PEARSON CORRELATIONS	SYSTEM CRITICISM		LEGISLATION-CRITICISM. IN FAVOR OF PROHIBITION AND PUNISH-MENT		LEGISLATION-CRITICISM. IN FAVOR OF SUPPORT AND LEGAL-IZATION		ACCEPTANCE OF THE JUSTICE SYSTEM		CAUSES OF BECOMING A CRIMINAL. PSYCHO-LOGICAL ONES		CAUSES OF BECOMING A CRIMINAL. SOCIAL ONES		CAUSES OF BECOMING A CRIMINAL. EXTERNAL CONTROL		CRIME PREVENTION. IMPROVED CIRCUM-STANCES		CRIME PREVENTION. TIGHTENING AND DETERRENCE		BELIEF IN A JUST WORLD. GENERAL		BELIEF IN A JUST WORLD. PERSONAL		SYSTEM JUSTI-FICATION	
	2010	*2018*	*2010*	*2018*	*2010*	*2018*	*2010*	*2018*	*2010*	*2018*	*2010*	*2018*	*2010*	*2018*	*2010*	*2018*	*2010*	*2018*	*2010*	*2018*	*2010*	*2018*	*2010*	*2018*
Causes of becoming a criminal. Social ones	0.024	0.135	0.037	0.121	0.031	−0.035	−0.008	−0.070	0.424	0.623	1	1	0.347	0.667	0.291	0.213	0.198	0.151	0.128	0.032	0.078	0.021	−0.044	−0.112
Causes of becoming a criminal. External control	0.014	0.131	0.057	0.026	0.097	−0.022	−0.119	−0.138	0.472	0.611	0.347	0.667	1	1	0.167	0.216	0.218	0.275	0.059	0.007	−0.031	0.031	−0.043	−0.107
Crime prevention. Improved circumstances	−0.095	−0.079	0.261	0.272	0.020	0.008	−0.009	0.107	0.113	0.170	0.291	0.213	0.167	0.216	1	1	0.231	0.299	0.114	0.081	0.026	−0.003	0.065	0.037
Crime prevention. Tightening and deterrence	0.052	−0.017	0.017	−0.078	0.326	0.292	−0.114	0.061	0.190	0.353	0.198	0.151	0.218	0.275	0.231	0.299	1	1	0.024	0.145	0.023	0.145	−0.108	0.150
Belief in a just world. General	−0.293	−0.323	0.020	−0.045	−0.092	0.117	0.453	0.384	0.168	0.138	0.128	0.032	0.059	0.007	0.114	0.081	0.024	0.145	1	1	0.614	0.703	0.487	0.534
Belief in a just world. Personal	−0.232	−0.287	−0.018	−0.118	−0.051	0.060	0.387	0.337	0.094	0.112	0.078	0.021	−0.031	0.031	0.026	−0.003	0.023	0.145	0.614	0.703	1	1	0.398	0.455
System justification	−0.336	−0.528	−0.019	−0.119	−0.128	0.119	0.469	0.576	−0.032	0.049	−0.044	−0.112	−0.043	−0.107	0.065	0.037	−0.108	0.150	0.487	0.534	0.398	0.455	1	1

10 Appendix

10.1 Questionnaire

Questionnaire number		Pollster's code:	

1 Which county do you live in?

Budapest	1	**C**songrád	6	**J**ász-Nagykun-Szolnok	11	**S**omogy	16
Bács-Kiskun	2	**F**ejér	7	**K**omárom-Esztergom	12	**T**olna	17
Baranya	3	**G**yőr-Moson-Sopron	8	**N**ógrád	13	**V**as	18
Békés	4	**H**ajdú- Bihar	9	**P**est	14	**V**eszprém	19
Borsod-Abaúj-Zemplén	5	**H**eves	10	**S**zabolcs-Szatmár-Bereg	15	**Z**ala	20

2 What type of settlements do you live in?

Budapest	1
Regional capital	2
Town	3
Village	4

3 What is your sex?

Male	1
Female	2

4 What is your age?

Exact age		Years old

18–19 years	1
20–29 years	2
30–39 years	3
40–49 years	4
50–59 years	5
60–69 years	6
70–79 years	7

5 What is your educational background?

Fewer than eighth grade	1
Finished primary school, vocational school, unfinished secondary school	2
Finished secondary school	3
College degree	4
University degree	5
No knowledge/No answer	6

6 If you hold a university degree, from what field is this? (several answers are possible)

Engineering	1
Science	2
Humanities	3
Law	4
Economics	5
Medicine	6
Information technology	7
Agriculture	8
Other	9

7 To what extent are you interested in topical social issues? (Card 1)

I have no interest whatsoever	I don't think I am interested	I am interested, sort of	I am definitely interested
1	2	3	4

8.1 Which newspaper or magazine do you read regularly? (several answers are possible)

8.2 Which one do you find the most credible? You can name newspapers or magazines you do not read regularly. (only one answer)

8.3 Which one do you find the least credible? You can name newspapers or magazines you do not read regularly. (only one answer)

	Reads it	The most credible	The least credible
Blikk	1	1	1
Bors	2	2	2
Magyar Demokrata	3	3	3
HVG (Heti Világgazdaság)	4	4	4
Magyar Hírlap	5	5	5
Lokál	6	6	6
Magyar idők	7	7	7
Magyar Narancs	8	8	8
Népszava	9	9	9

	Reads it	The most credible	The least credible
Story	10	10	10
Szabad Föld	11	11	11
Other	12	12	12
I do not read newspaper or magazines	13	13	13

9.1 Which television channel's news program or political show do you watch? (several answers are possible)
9.2 Which one do you find the most credible? You can name channels you do not watch regularly. (only one answer)
9.3 Which one do you find the least credible? You can name channels you do not watch regularly. (only one answer)

	Watches it	The most credible	The least credible
MTV1/M1	1	1	1
MTV2/M2	2	2	2
RTL Klub	3	3	3
TV2	4	4	4
Duna TV	5	5	5
ATV	6	6	6
CNN	7	7	7
BBC World	8	8	8
Echo TV	9	9	9
Hír TV	10	10	10
Other	11	11	11
I do not watch television for this purpose	12	12	12

10.1 Which websites do you visit regularly? (several answers are possible)
10.2 Which one do you find the most credible? You can name websites you do not visit regularly. (only one answer)
10.3 Which one do you find the least credible? You can name websites you do not visit regularly. (only one answer)

	Visits it	The most credible	The least credible
ATV.hu	1	1	1
Figyelő.hu	2	2	2
888.hu	3	3	3
Hír Tv.hu	4	4	4
Híradó.hu	5	5	5
Hírstart.hu	6	6	6
Magyar idők.hu	7	7	7
HVG.hu	8	8	8

	Visits it	The most credible	The least credible
Index.hu	9	9	9
Kuruc.info	10	10	10
Pestis rácok.hu	11	11	11
Napi gazdaság.hu	12	12	12
444.hu	13	13	13
Origo.hu	14	14	14
Portfolio.hu	15	15	15
Mandiner.hu	16	16	16
Story Online.hu	17	17	17
Alfahír.hu	18	18	18
24.hu	19	19	19
Other	20	20	20
I do not visit any websites	21	21	21

11 To what extent do you agree with the following statements about Hungarian society? (Card 2)

	Statements about Hungarian society	Definitely disagree	Probably disagree	Probably agree	Definitely agree
1.	Hungarian democracy will not function as it should even in decades	1	2	3	4
2.	It is inappropriate to show interest in one's family only and nothing whatsoever in public affairs	1	2	3	4
3.	The standard of living was higher before 1989	1	2	3	4
4.	Average people can influence public affairs	1	2	3	4
5.	Political parties do not really serve the interests of the country	1	2	3	4
6.	One should vote because this act influences political decisions	1	2	3	4
7.	Anti-corruption efforts are necessary in Hungary because they will produce good results	1	2	3	4
8.	A strong-handed political leader is required to solve the problems of the country	1	2	3	4

12.1 To what extent do you agree with the following statements about legislation and law enforcement? (Card 2)

	Statements about legislation and law enforcement	**Definitely disagree**	**Probably disagree**	**Probably agree**	**Definitely agree**
1.	Prison terms in themselves do not reduce crime	1	2	3	4
2.	Abortion should be banned	1	2	3	4
3.	The death penalty should be restored	1	2	3	4
4.	Increased welfare spending would reduce crime significantly	1	2	3	4
5.	Harsher sentences would deter crime	1	2	3	4
6.	Mild drugs such as marihuana should be legalized	1	2	3	4

12.2 Now I read out statements about the death penalty. Please select the one that best reflects your opinion. (only one answer)

The death penalty is pointless because it is not an effective deterrent	1
The death penalty is unacceptable because the state does not have the right to take anybody's life	2
The death penalty should be restored because just punishment to fit the most serious crimes	3
The death penalty should be restored because this is the best way to protect society against incorrigible criminals	4
No knowledge/No answer	5

13 To what extent do you agree with the following statements about the justice system? (Card 2)

	The law is applied to influential people and ordinary people differently	**Definitely disagree**	**Probably disagree**	**Probably agree**	**Definitely agree**
1.	The Hungarian justice system is free from political influence	1	2	3	4
2.	Verdicts and sentences often depend on the personality of the judge	1	2	3	4
3.	Hungarian courts assure equal justice for everybody	1	2	3	4
4.	In today's Hungary, it is always a good idea to take legal action	1	2	3	4
5.	Lawsuits are pointless, only barristers profit from them	1	2	3	4

	The law is applied to influential people and ordinary people differently	**Definitely disagree**	**Probably disagree**	**Probably agree**	**Definitely agree**
6.	I find court decisions acceptable	1	2	3	4
7.	The law and justice often remain separate in legal procedures	1	2	3	4
8.	The law is applied to influential people and ordinary people differently	1	2	3	4

14.1 How significant are the following causes during the process when a given person becomes a criminal? (Card 3)

14.2 Which one is the most significant cause? Which one is the second most significant cause? Which one is the third most significant cause? (Card 4)

	Causes of crime	**Not significant at all**	**Probably insignificant**	**Probably significant**	**Very significant**	**First three causes**
1.	Difficult childhood, early family problems	1	2	3	4	
2.	Mental problems, personality disorders	1	2	3	4	
3.	Poverty, serious financial difficulties	1	2	3	4	
4.	Impulsivity, revenge	1	2	3	4	
5.	Educational problems	1	2	3	4	
6.	Aggressivity, one's aggressive disposition	1	2	3	4	
7.	Greed, the desire to get rich quick	1	2	3	4	
8.	Addiction	1	2	3	4	
9.	Social inequalities, lack of social stability	1	2	3	4	
10.	Irresponsibility	1	2	3	4	

	Causes of crime	**Not significant at all**	**Probably insignificant**	**Probably significant**	**Very significant**	**First three causes**
11.	Negative peer pressure	1	2	3	4	
12.	Media violence	1	2	3	4	

15.1 Are you afraid of becoming a victim? (Card 5)

Not afraid at all	**Not particularly afraid**	**Sort of afraid**	**Definitely afraid**
1	2	3	4

15.2 If you are afraid, what kind of crime do you fear? (several answers are possible)

Assault	1
Defamation	2
Harassment	3
Hit and run	4
Rape	5
Theft	6
Robbery	7
Fraud	8
Computer crime (e.g. credit card fraud, data theft, hacking)	9
Other (or no answer)	10

16 What do you think could lead to less crime? (Card 2)

	These could reduce crime	**Definitely disagree**	**Probably disagree**	**Probably agree**	**Definitely agree**
1.	The lack of unemployment	1	2	3	4
2.	More discipline at schools	1	2	3	4
3.	Tighter human communities	1	2	3	4
4.	Increased welfare spending	1	2	3	4
5.	Harsher sentencing	1	2	3	4
6.	Stricter laws	1	2	3	4

17 To what extent do you agree with the following statements about belief in the world? (Card 2)

	Statements about belief in the world	**Definitely disagree**	**Probably disagree**	**Probably agree**	**Definitely agree**
1.	I think that the world is a fundamentally just place	1	2	3	4
2.	People usually get what they deserve in life	1	2	3	4
3.	The important decisions that I personally experience are usually just	1	2	3	4

	Statements about belief in the world	**Definitely disagree**	**Probably disagree**	**Probably agree**	**Definitely agree**
4.	Usually I get what I deserve	1	2	3	4
5.	It is my firm conviction that injustice in all walks of life (e.g. workplace, family or politics) is exceptional rather than normal	1	2	3	4
6.	I am certain that justice will always prevail over injustice	1	2	3	4
7.	The injustice that I experience in life is exceptional rather than normal	1	2	3	4
8.	Most of the things that happen to me in life are appropriate	1	2	3	4

18 To what extent do you agree with the following statements about Hungarian society? (Card 2)

	Statements about Hungarian society	**Definitely disagree**	**Probably disagree**	**Probably agree**	**Definitely agree**
1.	I think Hungarian society is honest	1	2	3	4
2.	Hungarian social and economic life is in need of significant structural changes	1	2	3	4
3.	For me, “Hungary is the most beautiful place in the world”	1	2	3	4
4.	Most Hungarian political decisions are made for the benefit of the general population	1	2	3	4
5.	All Hungarians have chances to become successful	1	2	3	4
6.	General social conditions deteriorate from year to year	1	2	3	4

19 To what extent do you agree with the following principles of distribution?

	Principles of distribution	**Definitely disagree**	**Probably disagree**	**Probably agree**	**Definitely agree**
1.	I would like to live in a society where one’s income reflects one’s contribution	1	2	3	4
2.	I am in favor of flat rate taxation where the tax rate is the same for everyone	1	2	3	4
3.	I would like a just society where the equal distribution of wealth does not depend on individual contribution	1	2	3	4

	Principles of distribution	Definitely disagree	Probably disagree	Probably agree	Definitely agree
4.	I am in favor of progressive taxation where higher income means higher tax	1	2	3	4

20.1 Worldview. To what extent do you agree with the following statements? (Card 2)

	He/She sees the world as	Definitely disagree	Probably disagree	Probably agree	Definitely agree
1.	Individuals just can't shape the world	1	2	3	4
2.	Life is actually meaningless	1	2	3	4
3.	"The end justifies the means"	1	2	3	4
4.	If you really try, you can make friends	1	2	3	4
5.	I often feel lonely	1	2	3	4

20.2 What do you think? To what extent do you agree with the following statements? (Card 2)

	What do you think?	Definitely disagree	Probably disagree	Probably agree	Definitely agree
1.	Whatever they say, most ordinary people are worse off than before	1	2	3	4
2.	The kind of future we face, it's a bad idea to have children	1	2	3	4
3.	It is better to live like there is no tomorrow	1	2	3	4
4.	These days you don't know who you can count on	1	2	3	4
5.	There's no point in turning to public administration, they are not interested in the ordinary person's problems	1	2	3	4

21 How serious are the following environmental and social issues?

	Environmental and social problems	Definitely serious	Probably serious	Probably serious	Definitely serious
1.	Global warming	1	2	3	4
2.	Spread of new epidemics	1	2	3	4
3.	Terrorism	1	2	3	4
4.	Environmental pollution	1	2	3	4
5.	Definitely serious	1	2	3	4
6.	Probably serious	1	2	3	4
7.	Probably serious	1	2	3	4
8.	Definitely serious	1	2	3	4

22 How important are the following communities for you? (Card 7)

	Communities	Definitely unimportant	Probably unimportant	Probably important	Definitely important
1.	Family	1	2	3	4
2.	Neighborhood	1	2	3	4
3.	Workplace community	1	2	3	4
4.	Hungary	1	2	3	4
5.	The European community	1	2	3	4

23 To what extent do you agree with the following statements about the effects of globalization? (Card 2)

	Effects of globalization	Definitely disagree	Probably disagree	Probably agree	Definitely agree
1.	The Hungarian way of life must be protected against foreign influences	1	2	3	4
2.	Cohabitation with people from diverse backgrounds leads to a more colourful life	1	2	3	4
3.	Foreigners who want to live here should have only limited rights	1	2	3	4
4.	The interrelatedness of countries is a good thing	1	2	3	4
5.	Freedom of movement and residence is beneficial for everybody	1	2	3	4
6.	The presence of foreigners runs the risk of a higher crime rate	1	2	3	4

24 Please indicate the extent to which the following sentences are characteristic of you (Card 8).

	Characteristic sentences	Definitely characteristic	Probably characteristic	Probably characteristic	Definitely characteristic
1.	Generally I am happy with myself	1	2	3	4
2.	I don't think I can be proud of too many things	1	2	3	4
3.	Sometimes I feel quite useless	1	2	3	4
4.	I have never offended anybody intentionally	1	2	3	4

	Characteristic sentences	Definitely characteristic	Probably characteristic	Probably characteristic	Definitely characteristic
5.	I wish I had higher self-esteem	1	2	3	4
6.	Sometimes I envy others	1	2	3	4

25 To what extent are the following ways of thinking characteristic of your personality? (Card 8)

	Ways of thinking	Definitely characteristic	Probably characteristic	Probably characteristic	Definitely characteristic
1.	I avoid situations requiring a lot of thinking	1	2	3	4
2.	I enjoy situations which call for new solutions	1	2	3	4
3.	I like thinking about abstract issues	1	2	3	4
4.	For me it is enough if something works fine, I do not really think about the why and the how	1	2	3	4
5.	I often think about problems that do not affect me personally	1	2	3	4

26 How would you describe yourself? To what extent are the following ways of thinking characteristic of your personality? (Card 8)

	How would you describe yourself?	Definitely characteristic	Probably characteristic	Probably characteristic	Definitely characteristic
1.	I don't like uncertain situations	1	2	3	4
2.	When thinking about a given problem, I consider all possible solutions	1	2	3	4
3.	I have never been late for work or a meeting	1	2	3	4

	How would you describe yourself?	Definitely characteristic	Probably characteristic	Probably characteristic	Definitely characteristic
4.	I prefer to live an orderly life in accordance with clear rules	1	2	3	4
5.	I often make important last minute decisions	1	2	3	4
6.	I have never offended anybody intentionally	1	2	3	4

27 To what extent do you agree with the following statements?

	Statements about human nature	Definitely disagree	Probably disagree	Probably agree	Definitely agree
1.	It is important that one can obey commands and issue commands if need arises	1	2	3	4
2.	Everyone should know his or her place in a given hierarchy	1	2	3	4
3.	I prefer being told what to do to having to make every single decision myself	1	2	3	4
4.	Human can be divided into two groups: the strong and the weak	1	2	3	4
5.	Human nature is what it is, so there will always be wars	1	2	3	4
6.	One day it will turn out that astrology can explain so much about life	1	2	3	4

28 To what extent are the following descriptions characteristic of you? (Card 8)

	I see myself as being	Definitely characteristic	Probably characteristic	Probably characteristic	Definitely characteristic
1.	Extraverted, enthusiastic	1	2	3	4
2.	Quarrelsome, too critical	1	2	3	4
3.	Reliable, disciplined	1	2	3	4
4.	Irritable, easily offended	1	2	3	4
5.	Growing as a person, being open to new experiences	1	2	3	4

	I see myself as being	Definitely characteristic	Probably characteristic	Probably characteristic	Definitely characteristic
6.	Shy, quiet	1	2	3	4
7.	Sympathetic, warm-hearted	1	2	3	4
8.	Careless, unorganized	1	2	3	4
9.	Calmness, emotional stable	1	2	3	4
10.	Respecting traditions, having not too much creativity	1	2	3	4

29 Your marital status:

Single	1
Married	2
Domestic partner	3
Divorced	4
Widowed	5

30.1 Do you work? If yes, in what form?

Ask the following question only if the respondent has a spouse or a domestic partner (question 29, code 2 or 3).

30.2 Does your spouse or domestic partner work? If yes, in what form? (Card 9)

	Respondent	Respondent's spouse
Upper management, director or top management with six or more subordinates	1	1
Upper management, director or top management with maximum five subordinates	2	2
Self-employed white-collar worker	3	3
White-collar employee	4	4
Middle management, other managerial position with six or more subordinates	5	5
Middle management, other managerial position with maximum five subordinates	6	6
Business (co)owner, entrepreneur with six or more subordinates	7	7
Business (co)owner, entrepreneur with maximum five subordinates	8	8
Office worker	9	9
Travel job holder or service providing employee	10	10
Agricultural producer, fisherman/woman	11	11
Skilled worker, foreman	12	12
Unskilled worker, domestic helper	13	13

	Respondent	Respondent's spouse
Homemaker	14	14
Student	15	15
Retired, annuity holder	16	16
Unemployed	17	17

31 How much is the monthly per capita net income in your household, including salary and all forms of financial aid or benefits? (Card 10)

Less than 100,000 HUF	1
100,001–200,000 HUF	2
200,001–300,000 HUF	3
300,001–450,000 HUF	4
450,001–600,000 HUF	5
600,001–850,000 HUF	6
850,001–1200,000 HUF	7
More than 1200,000 HUF	8
No knowledge/no answer	9

32 Which of the following statements is the most accurate description of your financial situation? (Card 11)

I can afford essentially everything	1
I do relatively well, but I am aware of my limits	2
There are things I can't afford, I run out of money by the end of the month	3
I am in a difficult financial situation	4

33 On a typical day, how many hours do you spend online for business and non-business purposes?

Internet usage	For business purposes	For non-business purposes
Weekday (daily average)	.... hour/day	.... hour/day
Weekend (daily average)	.... hour/day	.... hour/day

34.1 Have you ever fallen victim to crime?

Yes	1
No	2

34.2 If yes, what type of crime was this? (several possible answers)

Assault	1
Defamation	2
Harassment	3

Hit and run	4
Rape	5
Theft	6
Robbery	7
Fraud	8
Computer crime (e.g. credit card fraud, data theft, hacking)	9
Other (or no answer)	10

35.1 If general elections were held next Sunday, which party would you vote for?

35.2 Which is the party you would never vote for?

35.3 Which party did you vote for at the last general elections?

	Would definitely vote for this now	**Would definitely not vote for this now**	**Voted for this last time**
Fidesz-KDNP	1	1	1
Jobbik (Jobbik Magyarországért Mozgalom)	2	2	2
Mi Hazánk (Mi Hazánk Mozgalom)	3	3	3
LMP (Lehet Más a Politika)	4	4	4
MKKP (Magyar Kétfarkú Kutya Párt)	5	5	5
MSZP (Magyar Szocialista Párt)	6	6	6
MLP (Magyar Liberális Párt)	7	7	7
DK (Demokratikus Koalíció)	8	8	8
Párbeszéd	9	9	9
Other party	10	10	10
Does not tell	11	11	11
Does not know	12	12	12

Thank you for helping us with this project!

Pollster:	
Date:	. . . . .
Settlement:	

Index

Locators in **bold** refer to tables and those in *italics* refer to figures.